MW01288632

Strength Training Revolution

Grow Bigger and Stronger with the 4-Step Training System that Redefines Strength for Intermediate-Advanced Barbell, Powerlifting and Strength Athletes

Andy Xiong

© Copyright 2019 by Andy Xiong

All rights reserved.

The contents of this book may not be reproduced, duplicated or transmitted without direct written permission from the author.

Under no circumstances will any legal responsibility or blame be held against the publisher for any reparation, damages, or monetary loss due to the information herein, either directly or indirectly.

Legal Notice:

This book is copyright protected. This is only for personal use. You cannot amend, distribute, sell, use, quote or paraphrase any part or the content within this book without the consent of the author.

Disclaimer Notice:

Please note the information contained within this document is for educational and entertainment purposes only. Every attempt has been made to provide accurate, up to date and reliable complete information. No warranties of any kind are expressed or implied. Readers acknowledge that the author is not engaging in the rendering of legal, financial, medical or professional advice. The content of this book has been derived from various sources. Please consult a licensed professional before attempting any techniques outlined in this book.

By reading this document, the reader agrees that under no circumstances is the author responsible for any losses, direct or indirect, which are incurred as a result of the use of information contained within this document, including, but not limited to, —errors, omissions, or inaccuracies.

I would like to dedicate this book to Galen and Raymond for being some of my first strength training buddies.
I would also like to dedicate this book to Tommy and Zed for being two of the most supportive people in my life.

Cover designed by: Brian Du
Instagram: @briandudesign
Website: www.briandu.design

This book is available on Audible

www.andyxiong.com/audible/str

Also available on Amazon and iTunes.

Are you new to the concept of audiobooks?

Do you love books and literature but never have the time to sit down and read?

What if you can enjoy your favorite reads another way, perhaps while performing mundane tasks?

Audiobooks are a healthy way of structuring boring tasks.

Sex up what isn't sexy; try out audiobooks today!

Audible has the largest library of audiobooks – not for rent, but for you to own.

Contemporary new books, professional production, and quality narration...

Discover why Audible is the most popular audiobook service,

Get this book in audio for FREE with a one-month free trial of Audible

Table of Contents

Preface

In *The Greyskull LP*, Johnny Pain wrote that lifting isn't all there is to life. After proposing a 2-day per week training program, Pain wanted the reader to stop and think: *"Is strength training, or your time in the gym 'your life'? Is it what you live for*?" And if the reader had answered yes to either of those questions, Pain requested that the reader email him so that he can direct the reader towards a more meaningful and abundant life. Upon first reading *The Greyskull LP*, it got me wondering if he was right... but I never did email him: I just wanted to get strong, and *The Greyskull LP* provided me with a program to do that.

But today, I can now see that lifting is indeed a very small portion of life. In fact, being strong in the gym is not the same as being a strong person or being strong in real life. Dr. Oliver Sacks, neurologist and best-selling author who set the California state squat record in 1961 with a 600 lb beltless, sleeveless squat done in work boots, confirms this: In his autobiography, Dr. Sacks reflected on his weight lifting days, writing, "I sometimes wonder why I pushed myself so relentlessly in weight lifting. My motive, I think, was not an uncommon one; I was not the ninety-eight-pound weakling of bodybuilding advertisements, but I was timid, diffident, insecure, submissive. I became strong – very strong – with all my weight lifting but found that this did nothing for my character, which remained exactly the same."

Strength training may make you good at *doing*, but I didn't want to be good at doing. I wanted to be *strong*. Like, truly strong. I wanted to be good at *being*; knowing and having so much confidence and belief in myself that I can just be present and tackle whatever is in front of me, without hesitation and without second guessing my own abilities. This goes beyond being a good powerlifter, which is what most strength enthusiasts end up pursuing with their training careers. This is real strength. It's about being the best and most confident version of *you*. It's not about being the strongest powerlifter or the most technical weightlifter, because when you have a very strong sense of self you wouldn't want to identify as anything other than *you*.

But this is a big goal, and accomplishing big goals require taking a series of tiny steps. It requires the right strategies and taking the right actions. As such, the gym is indeed a great place to start forging this stronger and better version of you. In fact, if you've already been going to the gym, you're already committed to bettering yourself. You've already made the first steps. And it's not like traditional strength training or resistance training won't help... It's just a very small portion of both life and of becoming truly strong. Yet, there are so many people who aren't even strong in the gym. And if you aren't strong in this small aspect of life, how do you plan on becoming truly strong? The problem is simple: Far too many of you are prioritizing the wrong things in training. If you've purchased this book, you're already committed and invested to becoming stronger, but that drive is wasted without the right strategy and goals. Thus, I will reveal to you how you are training incorrectly and direct you on to the right path. Take action and you can master the gym while simultaneously master your life.

Note that this book is for people whose primary interests lie in training and not exercise. If you do not know the difference between the two, I highly recommend reading *Practical Programming for Strength Training* by Mark Rippetoe. For those of you who have read the book but need to be reminded of the differences, Rippetoe defines exercise as "physical activity for its own sake; a workout done for the effect it produces today, during the workout or right after you're through," and training as "physical activity done with a longer-term goal in mind, the constituent workouts of which are specifically designed to produce that goal." He adds that, "training is how athletes prepare to win, and how all motivated people approach physical preparation."

Since this book is about *training* and not *exercise*, everything in this book is designed to help you win – whether a powerlifting meet, a bet against your training buddies to see who can reach a certain milestone first, or an uphill battle against the obstacles and setbacks that prevent you from becoming a better and more confident version of you. But you cannot win if you do not put in the work. Today, I see an increasing number of people who claim training too hard will result in "raising cortisol levels" and overtraining. These are nothing but excuses. In the foreword of Jonathon M. Sullivan's *The Barbell Prescription: Strength Training After 40,* Nassim Nicholas Taleb wrote, "when it comes to physical training, there is no point engaging in the time-consuming repetitive replication of an active environment and its daily grind, unless you need to do so for the realism, therapy, or pleasure. Just calibrate to the extreme and work your way down from there." Note that advice is targeted towards the population that is *greater than 40 years old,* so what valid excuses against working hard do you younglings have?

For most lifters, the greatest benefit of this book will be in helping you assess just how advanced you truly are so that you can revert to a training scheme more proper to your level, identifying your weaknesses and what you need to work on, and providing you with a training system that trains all facets of strength. There has been much debate over what makes someone a beginner, intermediate and advanced lifter, and how lifters of each classification should train, even despite all the information already out there on the subject.

Even Mehdi from StrongLifts 5x5 has told me that the two biggest mistakes he sees are 1) people classifying themselves as far more advanced than they really are and 2) people who are beyond the beginner level continue to run beginner programs. This book will attempt to remedy that and more. But if you partake primarily in exercise and not training, this book will unlikely be beneficial to you.

Introduction

Today, strength training can be thought of as increasing your 1-rep maxes, and specifically only for the slow lifts which consist of the back squat, bench press, deadlift and overhead press. But real strength is more than having a high 1-rep max or a big lifting total. Although the slow lifts were originally popularized by York Barbell in the 1930s, with the advent of the Internet and the increasing need for physical activity it is strength coaches like Mark Rippetoe, Jim Wendler and Mehdi from StrongLifts 5x5 that really brought training the slow lifts into the limelight. And since powerlifting includes 3 of the 4 slow lifts as competition lifts, both the slow lifts and the sport of powerlifting, and subsequently maxing out, are becoming increasingly popular. In other words, strength as defined by your 1-rep max or your total is a *trend*. Despite this, it is also a revolution that redefined resistance training, and it is taking the world by storm.

In fact, according to Greg Nuckols, the rising powerlifting totals, records and standards aren't because of advances in drugs, supplements or training, but because of a bigger and bigger pool of participants. While playing around with data from powerlifting meets held by USA Powerlifting (USAPL), the national affiliate for the International Powerlifting Federation (IPF), the gold-standard of drug-tested powerlifting, Nuckols noted that "powerlifting, on the whole, probably isn't improving all that much. The typical lifter today is about as good as the typical lifter 5 years ago ([as] means and standard deviations are almost identical). However, since there are more people in the sport, there are simply more people who can lift at a very elite level. I.e. the average level of strength among the top 1% of lifters is relatively flat, but the top 1% of lifters (raw, male, open division) represented only 7-8 people in 2012, and 47 people in 2016." [1]

At the forefront of this strength training revolution are Rippetoe, whose best-selling book *Starting Strength: Basic Barbell Training* has sold over 300,000 copies, and StrongLifts 5x5, whose email list exceeds 200,000 people. And according to Rippetoe, the goal of strength training is to ultimately increase the production of force, which Dr. Austin Baraki of Barbell Medicine agrees with despite Barbell Medicine's split from Starting Strength in 2018. [2]

However, within the first chapter of *Strong Enough? Thoughts on Thirty Years of Barbell Training*, Rippetoe wrote: "I look back to 1961 and I see clearly that strength means way more than the ability to generate force against a resistance. It has always meant capability," and "its acquisition has always improved the acquirer in more ways than intended." Dr. Tudor Bompa, the father of modern sports periodization, has shown this to be true. Dr. Bompa revealed that strength training, when periodized, is superior to yearlong power training for the purposes of improving power capability, primarily because power is a function of maximum strength. In fact, Dr. Bompa credits this critical insight into the relationship between power and maximum strength as the key to developing nationally ranked javelin thrower Mihaela Peneş into the 1964 Olympic champion. Having improved her already impressive javelin throw by 15 meters within a year and a half of training, Dr. Bompa stated, "While speed has more genetic limitations than strength, I had decided to look for improved power by increasing maximum strength to the highest possible levels." [3] Thus, it is true that strength had always meant capability.

But although strength meant capability, strength is also *specific*. Dr. Chris Beardsley, a leading strength and conditioning researcher, even named his strength training book after the ubiquitous phrase "strength is specific." But this emphasis on specificity is also what pressured me to write this book: If you were to browse forums today about a topic such as increasing your bench press, the solution is generally to bench press *more*. Similarly, if you ask about bringing up a weak back squat, people will generally tell you not to front squat but instead do *more* back squats and *more* frequently. Does it work? Of course it works — strength is specific after all: If you want to get good at something, you will have to do it more. But that doesn't mean that it is the *only* solution or that it is the optimal solution. In fact, obtaining strength this way may help your ability to generate force against resistance, *but it will do very little for your character and who you are.* It is just too specific to lifting and too specific to strength as the ability to generate force against a resistance. These quantifiable expressions of strength do not represent what strength is actually about, which is capability.

And truth is there are other factors of strength that you can improve on instead of specificity. More importantly, **you are only as strong as your weakest link**. Neglecting these other factors of strength will not benefit you, but only hold you back. You can master the sumo deadlift, executing it with utmost proficiency and technical prowess, but that doesn't necessarily make you are a strong person – it just means that you are great at sumo deadlifts, and probably great at the sport of powerlifting too if your squat and bench are on par. But why stop there? If you identify yourself as a powerlifter, sure that's great, but what if you take away all the quantifiable measures of strength, such as 1-rep maxes and the sport of powerlifting? Are you still strong then? Heck, some strength sports, like strongman competitions, don't even allow sumo deadlifts. And when strength is defined as such, as the ability to generate force against a resistance, it requires you to tie your identity to *something* – and that in itself is a sign of weakness.

Redefine Strength Training for Carryover to Your Character and Your Life

Right now, all the focus is on neuromuscular efficiency in the world of barbell and strength training, simply because everyone defines strength as the ability to generate force against a resistance. This means higher frequencies, grinding fewer reps, and training at lower rep ranges and higher percentage loads; only because this is what powerlifting meets and maxing out calls for. And as long as we associate strength with a big 1-rep max or being strong at individual lifts or individual sports, strength will always be specific. But as you should now know, there are other factors of strength besides the technical aspect. Thus, *strength training shouldn't be specific just because strength is specific*. Instead, we need to redefine strength training for maximum carryover into other sports, to your character and to your life. Why? Because at the end of the day, you are not *just* a strength athlete or *just* a strength trainee; you are not *just* a powerlifter, *just* a strongman competitor or *just* a Crossfit athlete; **you are you**. And for *you* to be truly strong you have to be adaptable and capable. It's survival of the fittest, not the strongest.

Specificity and technical mastery is not about adaptability; it's about specialization and, more importantly, it's about doing. That doesn't mean that specificity and technical mastery doesn't matter though; there are just other factors of strength with even more carryover potential than specificity and technical prowess. These other factors of strength relate more to capability and *being* than they do to the ability to generate force against a resistance and *doing*. In other words, if you take away quantifiable measures of strength, these other factors of strength will still be able to help you whereas specificity and technique may not. It's like mastering the sumo deadlift only to have sumo deadlifts banned or to have barbells replaced by the trap bar. While specificity may no longer be able to help you, there are two other factors of strength that *can*.

The first factor of strength with more carryover potential than specificity and neuromuscular efficiency, which is the factor of strength that governs technical prowess, is mass and size. Weight classes exist for a reason: Size and height matters. The bigger you are the more absolute strength you have. The formula for force is *mass* times acceleration after all. And it is evident in all strength sports with weight classes that the heavier weight classes tend to put up more weight than the lighter ones. Just look at Olympic weightlifting, powerlifting and strongman. Similarly, even combat sports like Ultimate Fighting Championship (UFC) have adopted weight classes. But what about sports without weight classes, like Crossfit? Well, too much size can be detrimental, but one thing is for certain: Musculature matters. That's because, as Mark Rippetoe explained in his book *Practical Programming for Strength Training*, building muscle requires a real physiological change. Unlike endurance efforts which don't build new muscle tissues but tune existing ones, a real change in physiology is a change that actually sticks with you. It's not what you do because it *is* you. And unlike technical specificity where you primarily develop the neuromuscular system to be more efficient only at certain movements, you can apply this change in physiology in many different ways. Mastering the sumo deadlift may make you stronger at the sumo deadlift, but growing and strengthening your glutes will help you in multiple lifts, correct your posture and can even fix your nagging knee pain.

The second factor of strength with more carryover potential than specificity and neuromuscular efficiency is the development of the mental aspect that comes with any serious training endeavors. It includes things like the willpower to grind out a rep and resilience to pain, such as Wim Hof's ability to withstand extreme cold. Generally, the mind gives out before the body, so strength training should develop mental strength as much as it develops physical strength. But if you take the highly specialized approach of only training neuromuscular efficiency, say for example through the modified Bulgarian method of squatting singles every day, you don't build the ability to grind out reps because the program actually calls for you to avoid grinding reps. In fact, most high frequency strength programs require you to avoid grinding reps. The result is that you don't train the ability to grind at all. At the end of the day, strength training is all about overcoming challenges – and training plateaus are only one of *many* challenges that we can overcome. Getting that one extra rep or pushing through lactate build up are also ways to overcome challenges in training, and doing so successfully will build mental strength.

Of course, that's not to say that specificity and neuromuscular efficiency are unimportant. They are important, though more so for *lifting* than they are for *living*. Yet, so many people treat them like they are the only factors of strength because of how the define strength – as the ability to produce force, specifically in a 1-rep max. Before we cover how we can manipulate these factors of strength through strength training though, let's touch on the factors of strength we *can't* change and figure out what *can* be done about them in the next chapter. Read on.

Chapter 1:

Genetics – The Unchangeable Factors of Strength and Force Production

Depending who you ask there are 5 to 6 fundamental factors of strength and force production. Yet, all the attention is on technical mastery and maximizing neuromuscular efficiency through training specificity. In reality, you should be training all factors of strength so that you can become truly strong. Unfortunately, not all 5 or 6 factors of strength can be influenced by training. Thus, let's take a look at the 2 to 3 factors of strength that cannot be modified with training first, and see what we *can* do about them. We will be looking at Greg Nuckols's 6 factors of force production, as well as the 5 fundamental factors of force production that make up Barbell Medicine's general model of training. [2][4]

Muscle Origin and Insertion Points

Every muscle belly has an origin and an insertion point. How far these points attach from a joint can impact your strength. The farther out a muscle attaches to a joint the more torque it can generate with less work. For example, consider your biceps. Your biceps consist of two muscles, both of which originate from around your scapula and shoulder region. Both muscles attach to a bone in your forearm called the radius. Now imagine if your biceps attached midway into your forearm; it would take much almost zero effort for you to perform elbow flexion (the curling motion), even when holding onto a very heavy dumbbell. In fact, the brachialis, a muscle on your humerus that crosses only the elbow joint and not the shoulder joint, is actually the strongest elbow flexor – not the biceps. This is due to the fact that the brachialis attaches so far from the shoulder joint, allowing it to generate a lot more torque at the elbow with a lot less energy than the biceps.

Unfortunately, you don't have any control over where your muscles originate or insert. In the Barbell Medicine model, muscle origin and insertion points fall under the same category as the next factor of strength, because the differences are usually marginal within the human species. In other words, all muscles *will* have the same origin and insertion points in humans, but how shallow or deep they insert may vary. Thus, the Barbell Medicine model has 5 fundamental factors of strength because Barbell Medicine groups muscle origin and insertion points with segment lengths and anthropometry. [2]

Anthropometry, Bone Anatomy and Segment Lengths

How your bones are shaped and the lengths of your limbs can have a huge impact on your strength. For example, consider the Dalmatian and Celtic hip structures. The Dalmatian hip can be identified by swallow hip sockets which are great for deep ass-to-grass squats but are more prone to hip socket dislocation. This is because a shallow hip socket allows the femur bones greater ranges of motion. On the contrary, a Celtic hip is one where the hip sockets are very deep. Celtic hips are great for rotational power in a standing position, but are poor at producing power in the bottom of a squat. As a result, the best Olympic weightlifters are oftentimes those with Dalmatian hips because both Olympic lifts, the snatch and the clean, require being able to catch heavy loads in the bottom of the squat. This is evident in the sport too: The best Olympic weightlifters often come from countries with the Dalmatian hip structure, such as Poland and Bulgaria.

As another example of how anthropometry can affect strength, consider the segment length of your limbs. For example, consider powerlifters with very long arms relative to their bodies such as Cailer Woolam and Lamar Gant (who still holds a 634 lb record deadlift at a bodyweight of 123 lbs from 1980); their hands literally rest right above their knees. These powerlifters have it easy on the deadlift, being able to lift more weight with less work due to the reduced range of motion required to complete the lift. However, they may struggle on the bench press due to having to move the barbell through greater distances compared to their peers (though they can offset this disadvantage with a huge arch). Just by changing the length of the bones in the arm, you can completely change the strengths and weaknesses of an athlete in their sport.

Muscle Fiber Distribution

Your muscles are made up of muscle fibers. These fibers can be classified as either Type I muscle fibers, which are more resilient to fatigue but reach peak power much slower, or Type II muscle fibers, which fatigue much more easily but can generate maximum power very quickly. All of your muscles have a mix of Type I and Type II muscle fibers, and the ratio at which they exist can impact your power output. For example, someone with a higher ratio of Type II muscle fibers will find it easier to perform explosive movements with that specific muscle group. Likewise, someone with a higher ratio of Type I muscle fibers in their lower body will be able to run for longer distances before their lower body starts fatiguing.

Like bone anatomy and muscle origin and insertion points, the ratio of Type I and Type II muscle fibers are determined primarily by your genetics – meaning you have little to no control over this factor of strength. This is what Dr. Tudor Bompa meant when he said "speed has more genetic limitations than strength." [3]

What Can Be Done About These Factors of Strength?

Truth be told, there's not much you can do about your muscle origin and insertion points, bone anatomy, segment lengths or muscle fiber distribution. Barring surgery, it is neigh impossible to impact these factors of strength and force production. In fact, it's better to not think of these factors *at all*. When IPF champion powerlifter Mike Tuchscherer was asked about his opinions on what natural or genetic gifts are most important for the sport of powerlifting he answered, "I don't know. Honestly I don't spend too much time thinking about it as it's not in our sphere of control." [6]

Ignoring what you have no control over and not letting it bother you is one of the secrets to living a happy and fulfilling life. But aside from being practiced by one of the best powerlifters in the world, it seems that there's another reason to ignore your genetics: Greg Nuckols has wrote repeatedly about how your beliefs can impact your physiology, both objectively and subjectively. [7][8] If you convince yourself, or let others convince you, that you have garbage-tier genetics for lifting, you will actually perform as if you had garbage-tier genetics. And if you continue to perform and train like this over time, your final results will be lackluster at best. Additionally, some of the previously mentioned factors of strength may not actually matter for your sport or for a certain lift. In fact, Nuckols has stated that muscle fiber distribution is largely unimportant for the sport of powerlifting and for generating force in general, as the difference in maximal force production is only about 4% between Type I- and Type II-dominant muscle groups. [4] The biggest difference appears to be how long it takes for the different muscle fiber types to *reach* peak force production.

Therefore, don't stress over your muscle insertion and origin points, your hip structure, your segment lengths or your muscle fiber distribution. Instead, convince yourself that you have top-tier genetics and you will perform as if you were genetically gifted. Your focus and training should be tailored to the factors of strength that matter: neuromuscular efficiency, muscle mass and states of being. And once you redefine your definition of strength from something quantifiable, such as the ability to generate force against resistance, to something a lot more meaningful you will realize that your genetics don't matter at all. In fact, these factors of strength are *very* specific to force generation and lifting. In other words, while the playing field may not be level for strength sports like powerlifting, *we are all capable of becoming extraordinarily strong and capable individuals outside the gym.* Once you realize this fact, you will stop worrying about how strong you are in the gym relative to others because, as Johnny Pain once said, your time in the gym isn't all there is to life.

Chapter 2:

The Factors of Strength and Force Production You *Can* Change

There are 3 fundamental factors of strength and force production that can be influenced with training and 2 of them have much more carryover potential than neuromuscular efficiency, which is perhaps the most specific fundamental factor of strength. If we continue to define strength as something quantifiable, such as being strong at a specific movement, neuromuscular efficiency will remain king. But if you want to be strong beyond one movement or one sport, and if you want to be truly strong, your training should emphasize the *other* trainable factors of strength too. But first, let's explore all 3 modifiable factors of strength according to both Greg Nuckols and Dr. Austin Baraki of Barbell Medicine: neuromuscular efficiency, muscle mass and states of being. [2][4]

Motor Learning and Neuromuscular Efficiency

Motor learning requires repetition and practice. Powerlifters and Olympic weightlifters practice their competition lifts a lot in order to perfect their techniques at heavier loads. At the highest levels of the two sports, world records usually go to the athletes with the most *efficient* technique. Neuromuscular efficiency refers to how efficient your central nervous system (CNS) communicates with your muscles. Higher neuromuscular efficiency generally leads to better control over the body through more precise movements and/or faster reaction times, hence why it is called neuromuscular "efficiency." According to Dr. Baraki, maximizing neuromuscular adaptation, including skill and muscle recruitment, will require "regular practice and exposure to heavy loads," as neuromuscular efficiency is all about specificity. [5]

By practicing movements with good form, we can instill good technique and therefore boost neuromuscular efficiency for that specific movement. With neuromuscular efficiency being one of the few factors of strength you have control over, it is crucial to train with good technique. Training with bad technique is like building bad habits, which can eventually make it that much more difficult to progress. Worse, unlearning bad form generally means relearning new motor patterns, and then priming your CNS for maximum efficiency with the new motor patterns. Executing good technique consistently is a lifelong pursuit, so you might as well get started as early as you can. Although you may be able to make faster short-term progress with bad technique, such as heaving your butt way off the bench during the bench press, that short-term gain comes with a much higher risk of injury. All it takes is one serious injury to set you back months, or even years, of progress.

Neuromuscular efficiency is all the rage in the strength and powerlifting world because of 2 extremes. At one end, beginner linear progression programs like Starting Strength and StrongLifts 5x5 work so well because they focus exclusively on motor learning to optimize neuromuscular efficiency. At the other extreme, we have powerlifting elites: These elites generally have every other factor of strength nailed down and must focus more and more attention on motor learning and neuromuscular efficiency in order to get an edge on their competition. But for most of us, we lie at neither extreme. Both extremes make up a very small percentage of the population, but they also happen to be the loudest. Beginners rave about the results that beginner linear progression programs bring them, posting online about how it is the only way to train; on the other hand, how powerlifting elites train are broadcasted to a larger audience due to their large social following. The result is the illusion that our training should revolve around optimizing neuromuscular efficiency, when in reality this couldn't be further from the truth.

Muscle Mass and Muscle Size

If you woke up 50 lbs heavier of *raw muscle*, do you think you would be stronger than you were yesterday? Of course! When all other factors are the same, a bigger and more muscular you will definitely outperform the current you at any feat of strength. Muscle mass and muscle size is one of the very few factors of strength that we can impact, so if you care about strength in any way, shape or form, there is absolutely no reason to neglect it. Knowing the direct relationship between muscle mass and strength, you would think that any strength training program should have muscle hypertrophy as a goal – but, in fact, most strength training programs do not. Instead, increasing muscle mass is seen as a by-product of getting stronger. However, unless you are restricted to stay within a weight class, it would be foolish to not pursue increases in muscle mass as more muscle means more strength. Yet how many strength programs do you see that actually put emphasis on bodybuilding? Aside from Cody Lefever's GZCL method, most strength training programs have you accumulating most of your training volume from big compound lifts and competition lifts – which are generally not the best or only ways to build muscle.

States of Being: Psychological and Physiological States

Your psychological state has an impact on your strength. Name just about any pre-workout supplement and you are likely to find caffeine as an ingredient. This is because caffeine changes your psychological state by blocking the A2A receptor which in turn increases adrenaline, focus, and power. Alternatively, mindset can also impact your performance: A defeated mentality when it comes to training will likely hold you back from giving it your all. And as we explored earlier, something subconscious like the belief that you have suboptimal genetics for lifting can actually impact your training results too.

Your physiological state also has an impact on your strength. Imagine completely depleting your muscles of their glycogen storages and then trying to continue your training. You will be a lot weaker and fatigue almost instantly. This is why sleep is so crucial for performance: Deep sleep is necessary for the body to repair itself. Over the long-term, optimal physiological state can also mean having a healthy percentage of body fat and being free of imbalances and injuries so that you can perform whenever duty calls.

Luckily, we have control over our psychological and physiological states. In the short-term, we can take stimulants like caffeine to aid our performance, and we can choose to train in an invigorated state. Over longer periods of time, we can optimize our physiological makeup by building a solid foundation of muscle mass that we can carry over into new movements and activities. Thus, proper management of your psychological and physiological states should be of utmost priority. Of course, while most training programs are written so that you can avoid overtraining, you still have to nail down the rest, such as proper nutrition and sleep.

In Summary

Neuromuscular efficiency, muscle mass and your psychological and physiological beings are the 3 fundamental factors of strength that you have control over. Whether you define strength as force production or as capability, these factors of strength are at play. How you define strength will bias you towards training specific factors. For example, if you define strength as force production, you will gravitate towards specificity and neuromuscular efficiency. But to be truly strong, you must balance all factors of strength – not emphasize one over the other. So, in the next chapter, let's discuss the specifics of *how* we can impact these factors of strength through training. Read on.

Chapter 3:

Training the Factors of Strength and the Problem with Specificity

Neuromuscular efficiency, muscle mass and your psychological and physiological beings are the 3 fundamental factors of strength that you have control over. Whether you define strength as force production or as capability, these factors of strength are at play. Depending on how you define strength will bias you towards specific factors. For example, if you define strength as force production, you will gravitate towards specificity and neuromuscular efficiency. But to be truly strong, you must balance all factors of strength – not emphasize one over the other. In this chapter, we will go over how to train each factor of strength.

Neuromuscular Efficiency, Technical Mastery and the Problem with Training Specificity

Neuromuscular efficiency can be broken down into skill and muscle recruitment. However, when people think of neuromuscular efficiency they tend to only think of skill and, more specifically, technical mastery. Dr. Austin Baraki states that "the neurological adaptations necessary to lift relatively heavy weights are best developed by handling relatively heavy weights... In other words, you MUST handle heavy weights to improve and demonstrate top-end force production using the muscle mass you already have." [5] Thus, to be great at lifting heavy, you *need* to practice lifting heavy. You will need to repeat repetition after repetition after repetition in an attempt to find and ingrain the most efficient way to lift said weight. Although effective, it is important to note that this is as specific as it gets: It is hammering at your goals in the most direct way possible. And because of this specificity, it isn't as transferable as the other 2 fundamental factors of strength. For example, muscle mass is always a variable for force, regardless of the movement; while mental strength can be carried with you throughout your entire life, even when you leave the gym behind.

ASPECTS OF NEUROMUSCULAR EFFICIENCY	
Muscle Recruitment	**Skill**
Responsible for creating movement via muscle recruitment	Responsible for technical prowess
Fast to develop, and is largely responsible for "beginner gains"	Slow to develop once technically proficient; almost incremental

However, the biggest problem with high training specificity is the fact that it is *too* specific to force production and lifting weights. High frequency training programs like the Bulgarian Method, Squat Everyday, Dan John's Easy Strength, and high frequency training methods like Pavel Tsatsouline's "greasing the groove," all emphasize training as frequently as possible and at rep ranges and intensities specific to your goals in order to accelerate motor learning. But each of these programs also forgo training in a way that builds the other factors of strength, such as grinding out reps, which build mental strength, and additional bodybuilding work, which can accelerate muscle growth. In fact, a systematic review and meta-analysis published by Dr. Brad Schoenfeld et al. in May 2018 revealed that higher training frequencies were only associated with larger strength gains if the increase in training frequency allowed for an increase in training volume. When volume was equated, higher frequencies weren't associated with larger strength gains at all. [9] Although this meta-analysis does not disprove the idea that high frequency training results in better technique faster via accelerated motor learning, it does suggest that technical mastery is not all there is to getting stronger.

Thus, the greatest benefit of high specificity training, which is attacking and hammering at your goals in the most direct way possible, happens to be its greatest weakness. Strength athletes who want to better themselves on the slow lifts are always hammering at the lifts relentlessly, time and time again, until they set a personal record. In other words, they are trying to optimize and perfect their technique through high specificity training *year-round*. But there are 2 reasons why this is wrong. First, what worked then may not work now. There is a time when your training should be specific, and there are times when training shouldn't be specific at all. It's why periodization exists in the first place; it was created to predict these training patterns so that you can apply what would work best and when. Secondly, in the words of Mike Tuchscherer, "technique doesn't have to be perfect for you to get stronger or avoid injury. It must be proficient. You shouldn't have major technical flaws or a litany of minor flaws. But small deviations here and there won't result in the world exploding. Sure, try to get better with time. Work toward technical mastery. But along the way, don't forget to lift heavier weights and get stronger." [10] If Tuchscherer, powerlifting champion and one of the best powerlifting coaches around, says that your technique only has to be proficient and not perfect, I'd listen.

More importantly, neuromuscular efficiency has another aspect to it apart from skill: Muscle recruitment. Proper muscle recruitment, unlike technical mastery, comes *fast*. If you are technically *proficient*, you've already milked most of the gains that'll come from neuromuscular efficiency. The skill aspect, the pursuit of technical mastery, is a lifelong pursuit that you need not worry about. And according to Greg Everett, national masters weightlifting champion and head coach for Catalyst Athletics, consistency is much more important than technique. You see, in the sport of Olympic weightlifting, there exist 2 styles of lifting: the American-style consisting of 2 pulls that emphasize staying over the bar and the Chinese-style consisting of 3 pulls that emphasize keeping the bar close. The American-style of weightlifting is explosive and powerful, whereas the Chinese-style is efficient and controlled. [11] Many weightlifters believe that the Chinese-style is superior and should be taught to all weightlifters, but Everett has found that "it's more important that a lifter perform the lifts as consistently as possible relative to him- or herself than it is to perform the lifts with a certain technical style." [12] In other words, having inferior or inefficient technique doesn't mean you are going to be weaker than others: Whether you are strong or not is determined by whether *you* are consistent with *your* technique. And despite the observation coming from the much more technical sport of weightlifting, it agrees with Tuchscherer's stance on only needing technical proficiency and *not* technical mastery.

At the end of the day, technical mastery is a lifelong pursuit. As such, there's no reason to try and take shortcuts by running high frequency training programs like the Bulgarian Method. But despite all the attention technical mastery gets, Nuckols is of the opinion that another factor of strength is most responsible for how strong you are: "Proficiency or mastery comes with practice. The incremental gains in neuromuscular efficiency that come with continued practice after the initial improvements when you start lifting aren't enough to explain the size of the strength differences between people." [4] And outside of the two extremes that benefit the most from neuromuscular efficiency – beginners, who make quick beginner gains via the muscle recruitment aspect, and elites, who make incremental gains via improvements in technique and skill – Nuckols claims that *muscle size* is the greatest indicator of strength and force production capacity, and Dr. Baraki of Barbell Medicine agrees.

The Best Indicator of Strength: Muscle Mass, Muscle Size and Muscle Hypertrophy

"The evidence shows that [the] strongest predictor of force production capacity is the amount of muscle mass someone carries – and this becomes even more true once basic neurological adaptations (e.g., skill and neuromuscular recruitment) have taken place. In other words, in post-novice trainees, the amount of muscle you have seems to make the biggest difference in how strong you are," wrote Dr. Austin Baraki. [5] Yet, hypertrophy literally sees no priority in strength training. For most strength training programs, muscle growth is seen as a by-product of getting stronger – which is absurd because muscle mass is actually a factor for strength and not the other way around.

Additionally, most people aren't doing enough bodybuilding work, or work in general, to maximize muscle growth. But what's even worse is that people are being told *not* to do too much or they will risk overtraining. For example, StrongLifts 5x5 calls for doing *less* when you experience training plateaus. [13] This give you the feeling that you're progressing again but, at the end of the day, it's a short-term play: Dr. Baraki states that building muscle "requires sufficient training volumes, the specific dose of which depends on the individual's baseline training status and current anabolic sensitivity. The only way to productively and sustainably train at higher volumes of work is for them to be delivered at an appropriate intensity that both allows for sufficient motor unit recruitment, but is also recoverable (both within and between workouts). This latter factor (i.e., being able to tolerate the necessary amount of training stress) requires sufficient work capacity [or] recovery capacity, which itself is trainable by training more." [5] In other words, you have to train with *increasing* volumes in order to build the work capacity to handle even *higher* volumes of training in order to further muscle growth. Muscle growth comes from doing *more*, not less.

Lastly, if you've read my other books, you'd know that building muscle also requires high intensity training, which builds mental strength too. Pushing through the buildup of lactate, or grinding that last rep of an isolation exercise, is a much safer way to fortify your mental toughness than it is to grind out one more rep of squats or bench presses – where failure can result in serious injuries.

Optimizing Psychological and Physiological States of Being

While Dr. Austin Baraki lists only psychological factors as a fundamental factor of strength, Greg Nuckols considers motivation, arousal and fatigue as acute factors because while "learning how to mitigate fatigue and manage arousal are good skills to acquire... they have more to do with how much you can lift today rather than long-term strength potential." [2][4] However, we've already mentioned how believing in something such as having inferior genetics can affect short-term training, which in turn can impact long-term results. [7][8] Thus, poor performance in the short-term *will* accumulate and eventually affect long-term strength potential.

Additionally, I consider physiological state of being as a factor of strength too. But what I do mean by physiology when muscle mass and genetic factors like muscle fiber distribution are already covered? When I refer to physiology I refer to having ideal body composition, as few imbalances and injuries as possible, good flexibility and good mobility. So while my nationally ranked Olympic weightlifting friend is against me practicing the front splits (because that range of motion is not required for strength sports like powerlifting and Olympic weightlifting), I believe that flexibility *is* strength: It is strength at end range. The better I get at the splits and the more flexible I am, the more resilient I will be to injuries. And while having a low body fat percentage may not be a factor of strength, I also believe that carrying excess body fat is not the best idea. Though force is a product of mass and acceleration, mass in the form of body fat is different from muscle mass, as increased muscle mass can positively affect velocity, a factor of power, whereas body fat cannot.

$$force = mass \times acceleration$$
$$power = force \times velocity$$

In terms of programming, I'd argue that the first goal of *any* training program is to avoid injury, not get stronger. It is important to take a negative definition of health and wellness before holistic and positive definitions, meaning your focus should be on getting rid of injuries and correcting imbalances before striving for fitness. Although most training plans are written with proper thought and programming to avoid overtraining and overuse injuries, people still do get injured. In fact, do you know what factor predisposes you to the highest risks of injury in the first place? Believe it or not, it's how you feel or, in other words, your psychological and physiological state of being. As you will soon see, Mike Tuchscherer found that feeling off, trashed or beat – whether mentally or physically – is the only factor that can accurately predict injury rates:

Once a year, Tuchscherer runs Project Momentum, a study that allows lifters to sign up for a free training program in order to test various ideas and concepts in real-world training environments. Project Momentum 2016 attempted to gather insight into what makes a lifter successful, and there were several interesting findings. For example, contrary to popular belief, bulking, maintaining or cutting seems to have little impact on injury rate, though it does impact absolute gains. This is rather shocking, as consensus is that you should do less volume when on a cut. Yet, the lifters that participated in Project Momentum 2016 were all put on the same program, regardless if they were bulking or cutting, and there appeared to be no relationship between being in a caloric deficit and rate of injury. [14]

Another interesting finding was that lifters who made large increases in workload saw larger gains, yet these larger increases in workload did not predispose them to injury. [14] Participants who made bigger increases in workload probably found it harder to adapt to the training program, though this could have been offset by the use of RPE (rate of perceived exertion), which I will cover in Chapter 7, to regulate training stress. As a result, those who made bigger increases in workload, generally individuals with a background of high load, low volume training, probably trained using lower loads and higher volumes on Project Momentum. This new training stimulus probably disrupted homeostasis enough to elicit a newer, greater training response. Dan John has once said that the world's fastest periodized program is to do whatever you're not doing, and there seems to be some merit here.

Lastly, those who avoided injury on Project Momentum 2016 had far better gains than those who didn't. Although this may seem like common sense, the most interesting finding was that those who felt more rested and recovered had a lower injury rate. So while training at a caloric deficit or making large increases in volume does not predispose you to injury, how you *feel* – your psychological and physiological states of being – matters the most when it comes to injury rate. And even regardless of injury or not, gains were much higher when lifters felt generally rested and recovered, though Tuchscherer does note that "those who felt trashed and beat up still produced good results, but not nearly as good as those who were better recovered." [14]

Thus, how you feel, your state of being, matters. And when it comes to preventing injuries, how you feel matters more than how little you eat or how unready you are for large increases in workload. Heck, even something subconscious like feeling genetically inferior can affect your gains. As such, it should be in your utmost interest to optimize your physiological state of being and protect yourself from self-limiting beliefs. Thus, you may need to make yourself immune to "nocebo" as Dr. Baraki suggests, or learn how to mitigate fatigue and manage arousal as suggested by Nuckols. But the best thing you can do is to live a healthy lifestyle that incorporates multiple facets of fitness such as resistance training, stretching, getting quality sleep and meeting your nutritional needs. If you want to perform your best, you have to feel your best, so don't overlook either your psychology or your physiology.

Don't Settle As a Fighter, Become a Barbarian Instead

Emevas of Mythical Strength, a strongman competitor and elite powerlifter, states that lifters who put a ton of emphasis onto specificity and technical mastery are similar to trained fighters from the game Dungeons and Dragons. A fighter is trained, "relying and dedicating many hours of practice in the arts of swordplay and tactics to become incredible skilled and proficient at the art of fighting," whereas the barbarian "just hits you harder and harder until you die," not based on training but "natural talent, ferocity, strength and tenacity, which only gets stronger the more they enter combat". Emevas adds that while fighters may appear more graceful, they can be disarmed. And once the fighter is disarmed, whatever he was good at *using* doesn't make a difference anymore. While a barbarian can be disarmed too, barbarians were never good at using whatever weapon he held onto anyways: The real strength of a barbarian comes from the fact that he is good at *being*. Emevas suggests becoming a barbarian, which means being "strong irrespective of implement, time of day, meal timing, proximity to warm-ups, caffeine levels, etc. Develop such a strong baseline of strength that being unskilled is of minor consequence." [15] This is what it means to be strong. Strength is not a quantifiable expression of how much you can lift. Real strength is a part of *you*. Strive to be strong, regardless of the lift. Be strong, regardless of the sport. Be strong, not because of the fact that you are using a deadlift bar, but because you *truly are strong*.

Am I suggesting functional training, Crossfit, or strongman training over traditional strength training and powerlifting?

With all the bashing I've made towards the high specificity training that is required for powerlifting, which is the end goal most strength trainees strive for, it may seem as if I am recommending you to drop traditional powerlifting and strength training for functional training, Crossfit or strongman training. That's not the case though, unless you weren't committed to pursuing strength in the first place! As you now know, you are going to need to commit a lot of time towards lifting in order to build a bigger work capacity. Mehdi from StrongLifts 5x5 made the observation that many intermediate lifters are addicted to the simplicity and quick workouts of beginner training programs like Starting Strength and StrongLifts 5x5, but if you are serious about progression you can't be one of these people: While your workouts can continue to remain short and simple, you are going to have to increase your training density.

But at the same time, I do think that it is a good idea to explore different sports and new movement patterns. You shouldn't be training with high specificity year-round. This is especially true if you aren't interested in increasing either your muscle mass or your work capacity, which can definitely hold your strength potential back. In fact, dabbling in new movement patterns can result in quick neuromuscular efficiency gains via muscle recruitment, making you stronger overall whilst also removing the feeling that you are unable to progress. But before you commit to any sport, know that you are going to need a solid strength base to be competitive anyways. In fact, when we get to classifying lifters in Chapter 5, I explain why it would be unwise to specialize in any one sport or one style of training until you are advanced. However, many different coaches and sports have different requirements for each training advancement, and someone who is advanced according to one coach can be considered an intermediate to another. As such, in the next chapter we will compare and contrast different training classifications, and decide on which classifications to use to determine whether you are an intermediate or advanced lifter.

But before we move on, let me say this: Know that around the intermediate level, which will be most of you reading this, you are *not* a powerlifter, strongman, or Crossfit athlete. You are you. You are someone who is trying to better themselves through resistance training, but you are *not* your vehicle of training. Only people who are insecure and want an identity to cling to will identify with how they train. But training is about becoming a better and more confident version of **you**, so clinging onto the identity of a powerlifter, for example, is no different than being addicted to a certain drug, abstaining from it, only to cope using another drug. Thus, feel free to dabble in new movement patterns and different sports, and train with low specificity, but **don't identify as anything other than yourself.** Now that we've gotten that out of the way, read on.

ANDY XIONG

Chapter 4:

The Gold Standard for Measuring Training Advancement

Each factor of strength has a place in training, and especially so depending on your training advancement. For example, beginner lifters who can continue to milk beginner gains and elite lifters who have already maxed out their muscular potential may benefit greatly from putting all their attention on neuromuscular efficiency. Thus, to have a greater understanding of how you should train and what your training should prioritize, it is important to know your training classification. To simplify the process, we can turn towards different strength sports with classifications already laid out.

There are 3 different training classifications that come to the top of my head: the strength standards set by Dr. Lon Kilgore and Mark Rippetoe, official powerlifting classifications and Michael Gill's unofficial strongman standards derived from national strongman competitors. The best standards to use are the powerlifting standards, but only because there is a lack of a better option. Powerlifting standards are the most developed, and there's a lot less *wrong* with them than there is with the alternatives. For example, many of you will be familiar with the strength standards set by Rippetoe and Dr. Kilgore, which categorize you into 1 of 5 categories depending on your bodyweight and your 1-rep max on the overhead press, bench press, squat, deadlift, power clean and power snatch. [16][17] However, it's not very useful, especially because Rippetoe went a lot more in-depth on classifying lifters by training advancement in *Practical Programming for Strength Training*. At best, the strength standards originally set out can give you concrete training numbers for each of the slow lifts to strive for, but they cannot be used to judge your training experience.

Powerlifting has its own classifications, with each federation having their own standards. Although the most thorough strength standards developed to date, there are many flaws. For example, powerlifting as a sport is not a true indicator of strength: How well you perform in the sport of powerlifting is an indicator of how competitive you are as a powerlifting athlete, as factors like cutting weight, peaking, and technical mastery matter a lot more than brute, barbarian-like strength. And even though the slow lifts may not be the best indicators of strength, powerlifting as a sport only measures 3 of the 4 slow lifts. Developing and judging full body strength based on only 3 lifts fall short of what many functional training experts and strength coaches recommend. The Wilks score used in powerlifting is also flawed, as it favors certain bodyweights. Lastly, the classifications differ in different countries, different federations and at different times. For example, the Canadian Powerlifting Union (CPU), Canada's affiliate for the IPF (International Powerlifting Federation), the gold standard for drug-tested raw powerlifting, has been steadily increasing their standards for each classification in the last couple years. The Russian powerlifting classifications you find on the web are also dated, despite being one of the most commonly referred to powerlifting standards.

Gill's strongmen standards aren't official standards by the World's Strongest Man, but are numbers that would make you competitive at the national and professional level. [18] Like the strength standards first published by Rippetoe and Dr. Kilgore, Gill's strongman standards are most useful as goals for you to strive for. As a sport, strongman is similar to powerlifting, but it is a better indicator of true strength as it incorporates multiple different facets of strength like muscular endurance. But unlike powerlifting, it is much harder to train for strongman competitions as the exercises performed in competition are much more varied. As a result, you don't train for skills in strongman; you are training for brute strength. Strongman is about being a barbarian, not a fighter. [15]

Though strongman as a sport is a better indicator of strength than general strength training and powerlifting, it is much harder to replicate how strongman competitors train. Some strongman competitors, like Brian Alsruhe, train primarily the slow lifts, with implements thrown in as conditioning work at the end of the workout. Others train exclusively with the use of implements. As such, even if we had solid standards for judging training advancement from the sport of strongman, how to go about training at each stage remains unclear. On the contrary, a *ton* of research has been done on both the sport of powerlifting and on developing better standards and classifications. Training measurements like RPE (rate of perceived exertion) and exertion load were born out of powerlifting and powerlifting training, as well as training methods like daily undulating periodization. Incorporating exercise variation into powerlifting training is not done for variety's sake as it is in strongman training, but done with a purpose to drive the main lifts up.

So although powerlifting training, where emphasis is primarily on technical mastery, is not the best way to train for barbaric strength, powerlifting standards are great for extrapolating data on how to best train based on your training advancement. It also provides concrete boundaries for what constitutes as a beginner, intermediate or advanced lifter. However, using powerlifting standards to determine your training advancement means that you are going to have to test your max back squat, bench and deadlift every once in a while; but that doesn't mean that you should be training those lifts year-round. In fact, it may even be beneficial to test the Big 3 over other exercises because most gyms have barbells, benches, and squat racks ready for use, whereas testing something like an axle press may not be a viable option for everyone. Although not the best indicators of strength, the slow lifts are also used by strength coaches to judge training advancement: And when we combine insight strength coaches have made into training advancements, such as Rippetoe's training advancement classifications in *Practical Programming for Strength Training*, with powerlifting classifications and training recommendations set by top coaches like Mike Tuchscherer, Boris Sheiko and Chad Wesley Smith, you can get a much more robust and detailed look at how to achieve your goals according to your training advancement; which we will explore in the next chapter. Read on.

Chapter 5:

Defining, Classifying and Training Beginner, Intermediate and Advanced Lifters

Each factor of strength has a place in training, and depending on your training advancement you may benefit from prioritizing one over another. For example, beginner lifters who can continue to milk beginner gains and elite lifters who have already maxed out their muscular potential may benefit most from focusing on neuromuscular efficiency. Unfortunately, there is no single classification or standard for training advancement that works best for identifying and training novice, beginner, intermediate, advanced and elite lifters.

Standards that categorize lifters by training age do not take into account training quality, or whether it was actual "training" or if was just a collection of random workouts. The strength standards developed initially by Dr. Lon Kilgore and Mark Rippetoe for *Starting Strength: Basic Barbell Training*, based on the relationship between your 1-rep maxes and your bodyweight, are also flawed; otherwise Rippetoe would not have come up new classifications based on rate of progression in *Practical Programming for Strength Training*. Powerlifting classifications are specific to the sport of powerlifting and only take into account the squat, bench and deadlift. Although powerlifting classifications are some of the best tools for judging training advancement, they do not address how to go about training in each "Class."

POWERLIFTING CLASSIFICATIONS		
Russian Classifications	**IPF (CPU, USAPL)**	**Wilks Score**
MSIC (Master of Sport, International Class)	Elite	500 Wilks
MS (Master of Sport)	Master	460 Wilks
CMS (Candidate to Master of Sport)	-	
Class I	Class I	420 Wilks
Class II	Class II	380 Wilks
Class III	Class III	325 Wilks
-	Class IV	300 Wilks
-	Class V	275 Wilks
Note: These Wilks scores are approximates derived from the CPU back when they used both Wilks scores and traditional powerlifting classifications.		

However, when we combine how strength coaches train their athletes with the detailed classifications developed for powerlifting, as well as recommendations for each Class from some of the best powerlifting coaches, we can get a much more detailed look at how to train according to our training advancement. Heck, there's even a lot of overlap that allow for us to piece training insights from multiple coaches into one cohesive training ideology: The classifications described by Rippetoe in *Practical Programming for Strength Training* based on progression rate agree with classifications laid out by Greg Nuckols, and also plug well into observations and recommendations made by various powerlifting coaches, including Chad Wesley Smith of Juggernaut Training Systems, Mike Tuchscherer of Reactive Training Systems, and even Boris Sheiko. This means that we can combine training recommendations from 5 different coaches to get a very detailed look into how we should go about training for each classification.

Before we proceed, I recommend heading to www.andyxiong.com/bonus/realstrength for a FREE bonus: Not only will you receive links to everything referenced to in this book, such as training programs, but you will also receive the contents of this chapter in a cohesive table. There is a lot of information in this chapter, so being able to visualize everything in one table will help you grasp, and apply, the content. Now without further ado, let's begin.

Defining and Training Novice Lifters

What's interesting is that novice powerlifters don't exist; only novice lifters do. As such, you won't find powerlifting coaches like Chad Wesley Smith, Mike Tuchscherer or Boris Sheiko writing programs for or training novice lifters. Not that this is a big deal though, as Mark Rippetoe has already revealed that the best way for novice lifters to train: Since novices lifters can set training PRs, or personal records, every training session, they might as well take advantage of these beginner gains and *actually* PR every training session. This is evident in most beginner programs like Starting Strength and StrongLifts 5x5. Because proper muscle recruitment, an aspect of neuromuscular efficiency, is responsible for "beginner gains" the novice stage is very short lived, with Greg Nuckols claiming that the novice stage generally lasts 2 to 6 months. [4]

Defining Intermediate Lifters (and Beginner Powerlifters)

Intermediate lifters, as defined by Mark Rippetoe, cannot progress workout to workout anymore and thus need longer training blocks in order to set PRs. Rate of progression wise, Rippetoe claims that an intermediate lifter should still be able to set PRs on their slow lifts at least once every 4 months. On the other hand, Greg Nuckols suggests that an intermediate lifter should be able to PR every 3 months, and adds that the intermediate phase generally lasts 3 to 8 years for most lifters. [4]

Powerlifting coaches like Chad Wesley Smith, Mike Tuchscherer and Boris Sheiko have training recommendations for powerlifters up to Class II that match training recommendations for intermediate lifters from Rippetoe, Nuckols and even Dr. Austin Baraki. As such, we can assume that the intermediate lifter is the same as a beginner powerlifter, which in turn would be classified as a Class II or lower powerlifter. According to the CPU (Canadian Powerlifting Union), Canada's affiliate for the IPF (International Powerlifting Federation), breaking out of Class II and into Class I requires a Wilks score of at least 380 for the Open Men's division, which would be a powerlifting total – the sum of your squat, bench and deadlift 1-rep maxes – of 1254 lbs for a 183 lb weight class powerlifter. [19]

POWERLIFTING TOTALS TO EXIT INTERMEDIATE / CLASS II	
Weight Class	**Powerlifting Total**
74 kg / 163 lb	527.5 kg / 1160.5 lb
83 kg / 183 lb	570 kg / 1254 lb
93 kg / 205 lb	605 kg / 1331 lb

So while strength coaches like Mark Rippetoe and Greg Nuckols define intermediate lifters based on their rate of progression, powerlifting coaches classify their lifters based on their performance. This is why there is so much discrepancy between people who call themselves beginner, intermediate or advanced lifters: Everyone is using a different method of classification to judge their training advancement. People who judge their training advancement through *only* rate of progression, for example, may overestimate their training advancement simply because they aren't able meet Rippetoe's suggestion of setting a PR once every 4 months. On the other hand, people who judge their training advancement based on training age may have never actually engaged in training.

As an aside, note that Wilks scores for each Classification were gathered around 2016, when the CPU actually listed Wilks scores for each Class. Currently, both the CPU and IPF have dropped the Classification naming convention in favor of qualifying totals, and they are in the process of replacing the Wilks score too. As such, the numbers used here may be dated. For current qualifying total requires, as well as how to calculate your Wilks score, head onto www.andyxiong.com/bonus/realstrength.

Training Intermediate Lifters (and Beginner Powerlifters)

During a call with Mehdi of StrongLifts 5x5, he told me that one of the biggest and most common training mistakes trainees make is sticking to a beginner linear progression program for far too long. In other words, far too many intermediate lifters still consider themselves as novice lifters despite not being able to set PRs every training session anymore. To Mehdi, they are addicted to the simplicity of beginner linear progression programs. But having been there myself, I think it is the fact that there are no standards for how far you can take a beginner linear progression program that results in people trying to milk as much gains from beginner programs as they can. Having met my friend Alex who was squatting an easy 355 lbs for 5x5 at a bodyweight of 150 lbs, I decided to continue running StrongLifts 5x5 despite having repeatedly failing the last set at 285 lbs for squats. But what I didn't know was that Alex had been training for far longer than I have, and that he was already an active person before even picking up a barbell, having competed competitively in many different sports already; whereas I was completely sedentary and inactive until a few months earlier when I had started going to the gym. Everyone is different, start at different places and progress at different rates. Don't make the same mistake as I did and assume that you have to milk a beginner program until you can, for example, squat a predetermined weight.

Justin Lascek of 70's Big actually suggests switching to an intermediate program once your beginner program is becoming too difficult. Why? Once the program gets difficult, your form will start to deteriorate, and continuing to train like this will result in you ingraining bad movement patterns or result in muscular imbalances that will be very difficult to fix later in your training career. As such, once you are no longer setting PRs on beginner linear progression programs like Starting Strength and StrongLifts 5x5, it is best to move onto intermediate programming.

And regardless of which coach or expert you turn towards, most of them will agree that training 3 times a week is enough for the intermediate lifter. Texas Method and Madcow 5x5, programs with a training frequency of 3 times a week, is often recommended for intermediate lifters by most strength coaches including Mark Rippetoe, Justin Lascek and StrongLifts 5x5's Mehdi. Likewise, most of Boris Sheiko's numbered training programs, which are actually written for beginner powerlifters (the powerlifting equivalent of the intermediate lifter), also have a training frequency of thrice weekly. Even Mike Tuchscherer suggests performing 3 full body training sessions per week for the intermediate lifter and beginner powerlifter, despite being a huge proponent of higher frequency training. [20] Thus, it is safe to assume that a strength training frequency of 3 times a week is enough for the beginner powerlifter and intermediate lifter.

In terms of exercise selection, you should be getting the bulk of your training from variations, or, as Tuchscherer calls them, General strength exercises. So instead of a competition back squat with a belt and knee sleeves, opt for front squats or paused squats instead. In fact, neither Greg Nuckols nor Tuchscherer suggests specialization at the intermediate stage of your lifting career. Thus, even if your goal is to become a powerlifter, your training shouldn't only be made up of the barbell back squat, barbell bench press and barbell deadlift. In fact, your training shouldn't revolve around neuromuscular efficiency or technical mastery, but on hypertrophy and muscle size instead. Even Chad Wesley Smith of Juggernaut Training Systems suggests that the biggest limiting factor of strength for the intermediate lifter is the lack of size, and this is echoed by many other coaches too. [21] In the Barbell Medicine Facebook group, Dr. Baraki wrote, "The evidence shows that [the] strongest predictor of force production capacity is the amount of muscle mass someone carries – and this becomes even more true once basic neurological adaptations (e.g., skill and neuromuscular recruitment) have taken place. In other words, in post-novice trainees, the amount of muscle you have seems to make the biggest difference in how strong you are." [5]

And like Nuckols, Dr. Baraki is also against the idea of dropping volume in an attempt to realize more training PRs: "Once we have someone who has developed the basic skills to perform the lifts, and has developed some of the necessary neurological adaptations in terms of neuromuscular recruitment, we need to get them MORE JACKED. This means that training volume per unit time MUST increase, **for everyone** (... which of course, requires a reduction in average intensity). Note that doing the opposite – reducing training volume, increasing training intensity, and eating more – is an **incredibly** stupid way to train for gaining muscle mass." [5] Yet, this is what most beginner programs actually advise, including StrongLifts 5x5 and Starting Strength, where both Mehdi and Rippetoe have suggested dropping training volumes and drinking GOMAD –a gallon of milk a day – in order to put on body mass.

Rather, when you plateau on a beginner linear progression program, switch to a higher volume intermediate program instead. Dropping the volume from 5x5 to 3x5 on StrongLifts, or 3x5 to 3x3 on Starting Strength, and eating at a caloric surplus unnecessarily may let you set some PRs in the short-term, but it's not a long-term solution. According to Dr. Baraki, "waiting as long as humanly possible before increasing someone's training volume and frequency means you are also 1) waiting as long as humanly possible to develop the necessary work capacity to 2) TOLERATE the amount of training necessary, in order to 3) stimulate enough anabolism and therefore gain enough muscle, in order to 4) keep increasing long-term strength potential." [5] Thus forget about putting on mass through GOMAD because it's not body mass that matters; it's about *muscle mass*.

If you do plan on training the competition back squat, bench press or deadlift, Greg Nuckols suggests keeping the lifts heavy, around 75 to 85% of your 1-rep max, and at lower rep ranges like 3 to 5 reps per set. [4] The bulk of your training should be made up of accessory lifts, variations, and bodybuilding exercises.

If you plan on competing, or just want to max out the correct way, run one of Sheiko's programs for Sportsmen, which include 2 months of preparation and a 1 month taper and peak. Note that even Sheiko's programs, which are meant for peaking and maxing out, also have a training frequency of 3 workouts a week, solidifying the fact that intermediate lifters and beginner powerlifters only need to *strength* train 3 times a week. Of course, you can still train, or perhaps the correct term would be *exercise*, on your rest days – and you'll probably need to in order to build up your work capacity.

Defining Advanced Lifters (and Intermediate Powerlifters)

As an advanced lifter, your duty is to specialize in your sport – at least according to strength coaches Mark Rippetoe and Greg Nuckols. In other words, *this is the point in your training career where you should start making the move from technical proficiency to technical mastery.* [4] Yet, most people start specializing in certain exercises or sports before they hit the advanced stage of their lifting career. As you start shifting your focus towards technical mastery, start to experiment with different periodization techniques, as you will now have to plan your training according to your sport of choice. Note that both Rippetoe and Nuckols suggest powerlifting as your sport of choice.

The advanced lifter is equivalent to the intermediate powerlifter, which include Class I Sportsmen and CMS (Candidates to Master of Sport) powerlifters. Mike Tuchscherer approximates that CMS lifters generally have a Wilks score of 400. [20] According to the standards set by the CPU, which doesn't feature a CMS classification, 380 Wilks is required to break *into* Class I and 460 Wilks is required to break *out* of Master. [19] As such, you are an advanced lifter or intermediate powerlifter if you have a Wilks score between 380 and 460.

POWERLIFTING TOTALS FOR CLASS I / MASTER / ADVANCED			
	Class I: 380 to 420 Wilks		Master: 420 to 460 Wilks
Weight Class	380 Wilks	420 Wilks	460 Wilks
74 kg / 163 lb	527.5 kg / 1160.5 lb	585 kg / 1287 lb	640 kg / 1408 lb
83 kg / 183 lb	570 kg / 1254 lb	630 kg / 1386 lb	690 kg / 1518 lb
93 kg / 205 lb	605 kg / 1331 lb	670 kg / 1474 lb	732.5 kg / 1611.5 lb

Training Advanced Lifters (and Intermediate Powerlifters)

While the intermediate lifter should train primarily for muscle size and hypertrophy, the advanced lifter needs to expand on their strength base as their frame begins to fill. As such, this is the point in your training career where emphasis begins to shift towards neuromuscular efficiency and technical mastery. This also means that your training will be *specific to a sport* of your choosing. For most people, their sport of choice will be powerlifting because it incorporates many of the slow lifts used to build strength. And depending on when your powerlifting meets are, you will have to periodize your training and plan ahead accordingly to make sure you bring your best performance on the platform.

It's interesting to note that, up until the advanced stage of your lifting career, you may not even need proper periodization. That's because periodization contributes much more to strength than it does to muscular hypertrophy, which the intermediate should be focused on. You could theoretically run the exact same non-periodized bodybuilding program for years and still build muscle, simply because the process of building muscle is a much simpler process consisting of far fewer principles. In fact, a systematic review and meta-analysis published in August 2017 by Dr. Jozo Grgic et al. found similar muscle hypertrophy from linear periodization and daily undulating periodization. [22] Another systematic review and meta-analysis published November 2017 by Dr. Brad Schoenfeld et al. that looked at 15 different studies also found similar hypertrophic effects using periodized and non-periodized approaches to training. [23] Greg Nuckols performed his own systematic review on the effects of periodization on training and, although periodized training did appear to produce slighter faster and larger strength gains than non-periodized training, he too concluded that periodization style does not affect muscular hypertrophy, primarily because volume is the main driver of hypertrophy, not training method. [24]

However, just because your goals don't revolve around muscle growth as much doesn't mean that you should decrease volumes drastically so that you can increase training intensity: You still have to increase work capacity, and continuously too, if you want to continue making gains. Muscle size is still a factor of strength, after all. In fact, many elite powerlifters suggest that the strongest lifter is the one who has accumulated the most training volume while also avoiding injury. As such, if avoiding injury is the most important thing when it comes to training, increasing work capacity can be thought of as the second most important.

Because emphasis is now on technical mastery, fixing weaknesses is much more important than it was in previous stages of your lifting career. Muscle weaknesses and imbalances can be detrimental to how efficient you are with your lifts and, unlike genetics, fixing weaknesses and imbalances is ultimately in your sphere of control. Renowned coach and elite powerlifter Mike Tuchscherer suggests a higher training frequency of 4 times a week, while Boris Sheiko suggests a training frequency of 3 to 4 times a week. [20][25] However, Sheiko's suggestion for training only 3 times a week may be because his training programs for Sportsmen classes, which include Class I lifters, features a training frequency of 3 times a week. Since Sheiko's recommendations are for peaking, maxing out and competing, a training frequency of 4 times a week for yearlong or off-season training may be more beneficial for most lifters.

Defining Elite Lifters (and Advanced Powerlifters)

According to Dr. Lon Kilgore, elite lifters make up only 2% of the general population. [16] In 2013, Mike Tuchscherer approximated a Wilks score of 440 to break into the elite level, but with the standards set by the CPU in 2016, we can get a more exact requirement: Elite lifters, which are equivalent to the powerlifting classification of Master or Master of Sport, require a Wilks score of at least 460 according to the standards set by the CPU and, by extension, the IPF (International Powerlifting Federation). [19][20]

ELITE POWERLIFTING TOTALS ACCORDING TO WEIGHT CLASS	
Weight Classes	**Powerlifting Totals (460 Wilks)**
74 kg / 163 lb	640 kg / 1408 lb
83 kg / 183 lb	690 kg / 1518 lb
93 kg / 205 lb	732.5 kg / 1611.5 lb

Elite lifters are generally competitive at the national level of powerlifting. In fact, to compete internationally for Team Canada in smaller events requires a Wilks score of only 420, while competing for Team Canada at IPF Worlds requires a Wilks score of 450. Elite lifters tend to have Wilks scores that exceed the minimum requirements to compete internationally, hence why you also have to place top 3 at Nationals in order to be considered for Team Canada. [19]

Training Elite Lifters (and Advanced Powerlifters)

Whereas the intermediate lifter's programming is hypertrophy-focused and the advanced lifter's is strength-focused, elite lifters have to focus on proper peaking and tapering. That's because poorly periodized training, tapering and peaking can either make or break a competition. In other words, elite lifters focus extensively on their *psychological and physiological states of being* as competition approaches. Aside from the need to always be adapting to heavier and heavier weights, and the need for increasing volumes, frequencies and intensities, training for elite lifters is highly individualized. As such, training elite lifters is beyond the scope of this book.

Your Strength Training Journey

Your training career will often start off with a beginner linear progression program such as Starting Strength, StrongLifts 5x5 or Greyskull LP. Though most beginner programs make use of sets of 5, such as Starting Strength's 3x5 set and rep scheme or the 5x5 set and rep scheme found in StrongLifts 5x5, sets of 5 aren't inherently special. Though both Mark Rippetoe and Justin Lascek claim that sets of 5 are the best for strength – being heavy enough to be challenging but light enough to avoid crazy high levels of risk, and also allowing for the coach to interact with the trainee mid-set – Dr. Michael Yessis, author of the book *The Revolutionary 1 x 20 RM Strength Training Program*, has suggested that the use of single sets of 20 for beginners can also work. Though Dr. Michael Yessis's recommendation for sets of 20 is often applied to isolation exercises too, going from 1x20 to 2x10 to 3x8 to 5x5 to 8x3, for example, is likely a better way of milking linear progression and beginner gains than going from 5x5 to 3x5. At the same time, you want to avoid the most common training mistake people make according to Mehdi from StrongLifts 5x5; which is being addicted to the simplicity of beginner training programs and running them for far too long.

When you've milked your beginner gains and have encountered serious training plateaus, it is time to switch to a higher volume intermediate program and emphasize bodybuilding and putting on muscle to fill out your frame. Since a systematic review and meta-analysis published in March 2017 by Dr. Justin W. Keogh et al. revealed that bodybuilding had the lowest rate of injury compared to weightlifting, powerlifting, strongman and highland games training, bodybuilding should make up the bulk of your intermediate training. [26] Additionally, feel free to explore new movement patterns and variations in order to avoid overuse injuries from, say, back squatting too much. Intermediate programs like Texas Method, Madcow 5x5 and StrongLifts 5x5 Advanced typically agree with recommendations set out by strength and powerlifting coaches for the intermediate lifter, such as a thrice weekly training frequency and sub maximal lifting. However, there often isn't enough bodybuilding work in these training programs. As such, it may be a good idea to perform bodybuilding isolation work on your rest days. Your rest days aren't meant to be days where you are totally sedentary, after all, and if you are serious about long-term strength potential you are going to have to put in the work it takes to build muscle mass. (I know for a fact some are already complaining about overtraining and "rising cortisol levels"; and if this is you, you now know why you aren't as strong as you want to be: You avoid hard work.) Of course, avoid doing too much to the point where your bodybuilding work interferes with your strength training – and the only way to know if this is the case is to trust your *feelings*. If you want volume recommendations for bodybuilding that won't interfere with your strength training, consider reading one of my books on muscle hypertrophy.

Once your frame is starting to fill and you reach the end of your intermediate career, start approaching the technical side of strength by specializing in a sport and putting emphasis on neuromuscular efficiency. Whereas you were technically proficient before, the time has come to now pursue technical mastery. Having tried different movement patterns as an intermediate lifter, you should have a good idea of what strength sport you want to specialize in. And should you ever want to switch sports, you will have an advantage over others because you have your musculature already built up. If you don't know what sport to specialize in, or need a program for year-round or off-season strength training, Jim Wendler's 5/3/1 is a great option. In fact, strongman competitor Brian Alsruhe from Neversate Athletics still runs a modified version of 5/3/1 despite squatting well over

600 lbs, benching over 500 lbs and being able to deadlift over 700 lbs. It is also a program with a strength training frequency of 4 times a week, which agrees with the recommendations from the strength and powerlifting coaches we previously covered.

Finally, as an elite lifter, you train exclusively around your competitions, putting all of your attention into periodization and peaking properly. At the elite level, training is highly individualized. As such, it is beyond the scope of this book, and I would recommend hiring a coach to program for you and to analyze your lifts.

You Can't Have a Forest without Trees

Your lifting career is like basic sports periodization as explained by Dr. Tudor Bompa, but on a much grander scale. Instead of one training cycle where you go through phases of anatomical adaptation, hypertrophy, strength and eventually realizing your strength potential by tapering and peaking, your training career will span multiple years as opposed to a couple months. Heck, it may even take 9 years for some of you to reach advanced. Though the above explains why most people do not get as strong as they want to be – because they avoid building muscle and work capacity and focus exclusively on specialization at the intermediate level, or they try to achieve technical mastery despite not having a solid foundation of musculature – it is a very high level look at how you should approach training. It can give you an idea of what training goals you should focus on, but exact strategies and actions remain to be explored. For example, as an intermediate lifter, your priority is muscular hypertrophy and filling out your frame with quality muscle mass. However, if you focus *only* on hypertrophy, you will find it rather difficult to get stronger. If you specialize in building muscle, training with only isolation exercises like a bodybuilder would, you might as well be a bodybuilder. Thus, despite knowing what you should aim for on a macro level, having such a high level goal does not mean you hammer at it relentlessly in the most direct way possible. The trick then, is to figure out how to approach your goal. In other words, you need to have a training strategy.

But before we get into training strategies, I want to emphasize again that once you are beyond the beginner stage of your lifting career you are going to need to commit a lot of time to lifting and building a bigger work capacity so that you can continue to build muscle. You can't be addicted to the simplicity of beginner programs like StrongLifts 5x5 and Starting Strength and expect to run them forever. The intermediate level is the best time to explore new movement patterns, so sticking a foot into new sports to build technical proficiency with a wide variety of exercises while you slowly build muscle is a great idea. However, the intermediate level is still too early for you to be specializing into a sport. But still, keep an open mind and try new sports: Because if there's one thing I want to stress to intermediate lifter, which will make up the bulk of readers, *you need to be cross training*. Remember, you are you. You're not whatever or however you train. You are not a strongman competitor, powerlifter, or Crossfit athlete until you actually compete. You are just someone who is bettering themselves through resistance training. Don't identify yourself as any one thing and hate another without seriously giving it a try. Don't judge a sport by its cover, or by what the general population thinks of it. Identify as yourself and make up your own conclusions on different sports and training methodologies by partaking in them yourself.

Read on.

Chapter 6:

Training Strategy – Identifying and Combating Individual Weaknesses

Although your training advancement can give you a good idea of what to prioritize, in reality only adding muscle mass or only working on neuromuscular efficiency may not be enough to make you stronger. For example, as an intermediate lifter, your priority is muscular hypertrophy and filling out your frame with quality muscle mass. However, if you focus *only* on hypertrophy, you will find it rather difficult to get stronger. If you specialize in building muscle, training with only isolation exercises like a bodybuilder would, you might as well be a bodybuilder. Thus, despite knowing what you should aim for on a macro level, having such a high level goal does not mean you hammer at it relentlessly in the most direct way possible. The trick then is to figure out how to approach your goal. In other words, you need to have a training strategy.

Goals and experience levels are mutually exclusive. Your experience level only determines how to best go about achieving your goals. But even within certain training advancements or experience levels, what's best overall may not be what's best for you. In life, there is no universal right or wrong: There's only right or wrong *for you*. So if you're an intermediate lifter that does not mean you specialize in muscle growth; it's about balancing all of the factors of strength, but with a slight emphasis on the one factor that will provide you the most "bang for buck" depending on your experience level. Should you not know what to do, or if you are truly balanced, you can then default onto muscle hypertrophy. So while your macro goal is to fill out your frame as an intermediate lifter, sometimes you may actually benefit more from, say, fixing your form.

Identifying your weaknesses and neuromuscular inefficiencies can be a very daunting and difficult task. But if we take a first principles approach to identifying the cause of your plateaus, as elite powerlifter and Olympic coach Robert Frederick did, it comes down to 1 of 4 scenarios: 1) You are weak with bad technique,

2) you are weak with good technique, 3) you are strong with bad technique, or 4) the ideal situation where you are strong with good technique. Simply put, lifters can be categorized based on 2 criteria: whether they are strong or weak, and whether they have good or bad technique. [27] These 4 scenarios, which I will unofficially refer to as Sheiko's Quadrants, as it is one of the basics of Boris Sheiko's programming, provide us with a huge insight into where we should take our training.

Weak Lifters with Bad Technique

The first scenario, or quadrant, is lifters who are weak *and* have bad technique. This quadrant is generally made up of novice lifters who are completely new to physical activity. However, people who have taken a long period of time off from training, and thus suffer from detraining, would also qualify. Like training novice lifters, weak lifters with bad technique will benefit from beginner linear progression programs where the emphasis is largely on neuromuscular efficiency and proper muscle recruitment to build or rebuild technique proficiency. While untrained lifters will benefit from huge beginner gains, detrained lifters will also see accelerated progress as they relearn forgotten movement patterns.

Weak Lifters with Good Technique

The second scenario is lifters who have great technique but are weak. Oftentimes, this is a lack of mental strength, resulting in the inability to grind through tough repetitions. Although neither Boris Sheiko nor Robert Frederick has commented on what kind of training would work best for this quadrant of lifters, elite powerlifter Ben Polkov suggests that emphasis needs to be put on building foundational strength, such as performing more sets in the 3 to 6 rep range, prioritizing front squats over back squats and deadlifts variants like the Romanian deadlift or the stiff-legged deadlift over competition deadlifts, and incorporating extra dumbbell bench work and overhead presses to bring up your bench press. [28]

In other words, weak lifters with good technique should incorporate more general strength exercises, as they are already proficient with specific, competition lifts. Personally, I would recommend incorporating what I call "brute strength" exercises, which are general strength exercises that are also safer to grind with. The front squat is an example of what I would consider a brute strength exercise, as it is much easier and safer to dump the barbell on a front squat than it is on a back squat. Not only will the front squat build up and strengthen lagging muscles like the quads, core and thoracic spine, but grinding with atrocious form on the front squat is a lot better than grinding with atrocious form on the back squat, primarily because you don't want to be ingraining poor movement patterns on lifts you are going to pursue technical mastery on. We will go more in-depth on exercise selection in Chapter 9.

Weak lifters with good technique can also take a more specific approach to getting stronger, one where you don't have to swap out your main lifts for brute or general strength exercises. All you have to do is learn to grind. As an elite powerlifter and head coach for Reactive Training Systems, Mike Tuchscherer has found that increasing the number of reps per set by 1 – but staying within the normally suggested 4 to 6 rep range – while simultaneously decreasing the number of sets by 1 will allow you to practice grinding. And because the total volume, number of lifts and intensity remains the same it wouldn't completely throw you off of your programming. So instead of 5 sets of 3 reps at 80%, opt for 4 sets of 4 at 80%. As for why it works, as well as why it can be superior to shifting your focus towards general strength exercises and exercise variations, Tuchscherer states that as the reps go by and fatigue starts to kick in, the lifter will be "spending more time under tension in their weakest position. And that time under tension is highly specific to the way that they will need to perform when they are doing a max effort lift. Doing more reps in the contest lift is a great way to bring up a glaring weak point because it teaches you how to strain by using fatigue as a benefit." [29] Though this training technique was originally developed for use with Sheiko's training programs by one of Tuchscherer's friends, it can be employed to other strength training programs as well.

Strong Lifters with Bad Technique

Certain training methodologies work better for certain demographics, like how beginners can make insane progress from building neuromuscular efficiency. As for Boris Sheiko's training templates, they work best for strong lifters who have bad technique. Robert Frederick discovered that strong lifters with bad technique generally "have a fair amount of training experience without ever being formally coached, train solo in the gym, and get the majority of their information online. The universal templates [by Sheiko] are thus written for this group. Lifters that have a good strength base, yet make common errors in the competitive lifts will get the most from the universal programs as written". [27] Personally, I agree with Frederick's statement as I was in that exact scenario when I decided to run Sheiko's 3 day large load intermediate program. My first time running it brought my squat from a sloppy 385 lbs at a bodyweight of 160 lbs to an easy 425 lbs, then to 440 lbs right after while barely missing 455 lbs – all at a bodyweight of no more than 174 lbs. If I had hit the 455 lb squat, I would have increased my squat by a total of 75 lbs in 6 months! Thus, it is true that Sheiko's programs work great for the demographic of lifters described by Frederick.

The reason Sheiko's programs are so effective for strong lifters with bad technique is simple: Sheiko's programs have a ton of quality repetition work. Not only is the total number of repetitions for the squat and bench high, but there is also minimal grinding and minimal deviation of form or technique. For example, in Sheiko #29, a 4-week introduction to the kind of volumes you would find in Sheiko's programs, you are performing a total of 342 reps of squats, 454 reps of bench and 185 reps of deadlifts. Of the 342 reps of squats, only a total of 8 reps are done at more than 80% of your 1-rep max; and for bench, no more than 14 reps of the 454 total. Compare that to 5/3/1, where you are looking at only around 75 reps per lift per month, with increasing intensities the more you run it! When you are performing this many repetitions, with no more than 85% loads and for no more than 5 reps per set, your repetitions are bound to be quality.

However, Sheiko's programs aren't the only option available for this quadrant of lifters. Theoretically, any high frequency program that places emphasis on neuromuscular efficiency can work, including Squat Everyday and Dan John's Easy Strength. Training methods like Pavel Tsatsouline's "greasing the groove" can also benefit this group of lifters. Why? Because practice makes perfect. In fact, a systematic review and meta-analysis published in May 2018 by Dr. James W. Krieger et al. that looked at 22 different studies on how frequency affects strength revealed that higher training frequencies seemed to benefit compound lifts, especially upper body compounds, the most. [30] This makes sense, as compound movements are much more technical, and a higher training frequency with emphasis on quality repetitions allows for more technical practice. As for the relationship between training frequency and upper body compounds, there are two reasons. First, the upper body is made up of more muscles than the lower body, but these muscles are also smaller. This smaller size means less room for muscle glycogen storages, which means the muscles fatigue faster and thus need to be trained more often. Secondly, compound exercises for the upper body, like the bench press and overhead press, are much more technical than lower body compound exercises because of the shorter ranges of motion. Thus, the pursuit of technical prowess, whether through training programs like Sheiko's or high frequency programs, will benefit strong lifters with bad technique the most. However, if you decide to run one of the high frequency training programs, make sure you are incorporating bodybuilding work on the side too. Unlike Boris Sheiko's programs where the volumes are incredibly high, not many of these programs are written to optimize muscle growth and muscle mass, which the intermediate lifter direly needs.

Strong Lifters with Good Technique

This is the quadrant you want to be in at the end of every training cycle or before you enter the peaking and tapering phase of your program. Getting to this quadrant is pretty simple: Train in a way that fixes what holds you back, which is either weakness or bad technique. When you are considered a strong lifter with good technique, the only way to go about training is to steadily increase your training percentages while decreasing volume. In other words, you are literally peaking and tapering so that you can realize your strength in a 1-rep max attempt.

For example, an intermediate lifter's macro level goal will be to fill out their frame with quality mass in the form of muscle mass. But on a more micro level, the lifter will fall into 1 of the 4 Sheiko Quadrants. Whilst still building their work capacity and attempting to build as much muscle as possible, the lifter must also strength train in a way that addresses whatever holds him or her back, whether that is weakness or lack of technicality. That's what training strategy is: How you go about approaching your goals. And when you have your goal and strategy figured out, all that's left are taking the appropriate actions – which can be something as simple as adhering to the right training program.

Mike Tuchscherer's Project Momentum 17-1

Mike Tuchscherer also found a similar trend with the results of Project Momentum 2017. Project Momentum 2017, codenamed as Project Momentum 17-1, was a free training program to test the claim that "lifters who can do low reps with 80% of [1-rep max] are fast-twitch dominant and therefore should train with low reps per set [as] that will allow them to progress the fastest." However, Project Momentum 17-1 revealed the opposite to be true instead: Tuchscherer found that lifters who are only capable of performing less than 8 reps at 80% 1-rep max benefitted more from higher rep counts per set, while lifters would were able to perform 8 or more reps at 80% 1-rep max benefitted more from low rep training with heavier weights. [31]

The findings from Project Momentum 17-1 seem to agree with the scenarios presented by Boris Sheiko and Robert Frederick: Lifters seem to make better progress by tackling their weaknesses and doing what they are bad at. In other words, lifters would are weak and are incapable of grinding out reps would benefit from practicing how to grind, as well as building up their strength base; whereas lifters with bad technique will benefit greatly from performing lots of high quality repetitions.

However, it is important to note that Project Momentum 2016's finding that those who felt more recovered and enjoyed their training also performed better in Project Momentum 17-1. As such, it can be a good idea to do things which help you *feel* better. In other words, if you need to build foundational strength but cannot stand front squatting, it may be a better idea to approach building foundational strength using Tuchscherer's method of increasing your reps per set by 1 while simultaneously decreasing your number of sets by 1. But if your back squat is being held back by faulty core strength, weak quads and weak thoracic strength – things that front squats can address and strengthen – it may be a better idea to just suck it up and front squat instead.

As you can see, there is no one-size fits all solution to getting stronger. Lifters in the same training advancement and with similar training experience may have the same goals to prioritize on the macro level, such as increasing muscle mass and filling out their frames, but what holds them back strength-wise may differ. In fact, both Tuchscherer and Reactive Training Systems (RTS) are all about training individualization, and their coaching results show: RTS has won multiple awards for being the best powerlifting team in the IPF. To Tuchscherer, every lifter is different and should train differently as a result. And fortunately for you, you too can individualize your training using Tuchscherer's training measurements like RPE (rate of perceived exertion), which standardizes training stress from different intensities and rep ranges, and TSI (training stress index), which standardizes training stress from different volumes. We cover these training variables, and others, in the following chapter. Read on.

Chapter 7:

Training Variables – Redefining the Old and Defining the New

As you become more advanced of a lifter, your training will become increasingly individualized. That's because traditional strength training variables, like intensity and volume, are flawed and do not accurately represent training stress. While they *attempt* to standardize and quantify training stress, many coaches have started coming up with new units of measurement instead. But what's most surprising is that these new units ignore things like how much weight is on the barbell and quantify things like how you feel instead. Although this may seem counterintuitive, Robert Frederick explains why best: On his website, Strongur, Frederick states that "volume load is an *external* measure of training stress, while effort is an *internal* measure. Internal measure is ultimately what drives a physiological response. Five sets of 200 lbs might be a warm-up for one person and an overload for another. This external load is the same in both cases but the internal load is not. The internal load is the one we really care about." [32] As such, traditional training variables that take into account external measures of training stress, like percentage load and volume, are outdated and need to be redefined or scrapped for internal measures of training stress instead. In this chapter, we will explore the various new training variables that top coaches like Mike Tuchscherer and Boris Sheiko have come up with.

Percentage Load versus Intensity

First, let's start off with percentage load and intensity as these are either the same thing or something completely different, depending on who you ask. That's because in this day and age, and especially so in the world of strength training, intensity is mistaken as percentage load: When a program lists an intensity of 80%, it actually refers to a weight equal to 80% of your 1-rep max – which is a percentage load. Load is the weight you use when doing a specific exercise. It is usually a percentage of your rep maxes, with most training programs using a percentage of your 1-rep max. In other words, intensity in the world of strength training, powerlifting and Olympic weightlifting actually refers to load. For example, an intensity of 70% often refers to a load equivalent to 70% of your 1-rep max on that specific exercise. But in the scientific world, where terms are strictly defined, these percentages are referred to as "loads" instead. High load training, then, is training close to your 1-rep max.

Intensity $\neq$ Percentage Load (%)

So how did the word intensity end up in the position where it describes load? In the bodybuilding world, intensity is a measure of the effort of training. Training with high intensity means training with the intent to overload the muscle. Low intensity training, like low intensity cardio, means low impact training. You can kind of already see how the definition of intensity shifted in the world of strength training: It is easier to prescribe the same load and rep and set scheme using absolute terms than it is to describe how much effort you should put into training. For example, as a coach, you can tell your athlete to perform 5 reps of squats at high intensity because you think that the training adaptations that come with it is what your athlete needs, but to the athlete it is vague and ambiguous. So why not just prescribe the exact load and exact set and rep scheme to get as close to the training response that you wanted to prescribe in the first place? For example, which would you prefer I tell you: Perform a set of 5 squats at a very high intensity, or perform a set of 5 squats at 85% of your 1-rep max? (Most coaches estimate your 5-rep max to be between 87.5-90% of your 1-rep max, so 85% for 5 is indeed high intensity *and* high load.) Many of you would prefer the latter because it isn't as ambiguous.

However, there's just one problem with percentage loads. Normally, percentage loads are prescribed with set and rep schemes to try and capture a specific training response or stress, but it fails at it because it does not take into account adaptations your body has already towards that particular stimulus. For example, if you've been performing a heavy single of squats everyday at 95% of your 1-rep max, singles at 95% will no longer be as challenging to you and will elicit a different training response and stress than if you were just starting to perform singles at 95%. In other words, the internal measure of stress will differ despite the percentage loads remaining at 95%.

Intensity, on the other hand, is actually an *internal* measure of stress, and measuring intensity would be superior than measuring percentage loads, especially for those who are interested in programming for themselves. Note that high intensity training is what builds mental strength, while training at certain loads builds technical prowess at those loads.

Measuring Intensity in the World of Strength Training

It makes sense to measure intensity, an internal measure of stress, over load, which is external. However, intensity is generally subjective, making measurements of intensity in the world of strength training hard to standardize. For example, consider the use of intensity in terms of bodybuilding and conditioning, where it stays true to its definition. Cardio done through HIIT, or high-intensity interval training, is conditioning work that is high impact and, truth be told, dreadful; and it is always more intense than low intensity cardio. In bodybuilding, there exists high intensity training, where every set is taken to failure, which is also challenging by default. But in strength training, this is not the case. Although many people may consider a training load of 90% to be high intensity, if you've been training at 90% a lot already, singles at 90% can be performed habitually and effortlessly provided that you've adapted to the stress. Fortunately, there is a way to measure intensity while strength training. In fact, training intensity is actually making a comeback, and claiming its true definition as effort, via Mike Tuchscherer's RPE, or Rate of Perceived Exertion, scale. In the Powerlifting Summit 2017, Mike Tuchscherer stated that "RPE governs intensity, and intensity determines the training effect."

To use RPE, imagine it as a scale from 0 to 10 describing how hard a particular set felt. A RPE rating of 5 is considered easy, while a RPE rating of 7 is considered perfect for speed work. A RPE rating of 9.5 is challenging, and generally means that you *may* have been able to perform 1 more rep. A rating of 10 would mean it was maximal effort, and that there would have been no way you could have done another rep. Do note that while Mike Tuchscherer popularized RPE and explained it using RPE charts, which show RPE as a function of different percentage loads and rep ranges, RPE charts are visual examples: As such, it would be a bad idea to transcribe a percentage-based program to one that is based on RPE, unless you are using an RPE chart that is tailored to you. Tuchscherer actually recommends you to fill out your own RPE chart, as incongruent RPE and percentages will result in intensities that cause a lot of fatigue. Fortunately, there is no need for having a RPE chart in the first place as it defeats the purpose of RPE, which is *training based on how you feel.*

$$RPE \neq RIR$$

Sometimes, RPE is mistaken as RIR, or Reps in Reserve, but the two are completely different. To understand why, you must understand how to use RIR. A RIR of 1 rep means that you likely could have done 1 more rep; whereas a RIR of 2-3 means that you *may* have been able to do 2 to 3 more repetitions. While many people believe that RIR is simply 10 minus RPE, it simply isn't true either. Like how intensity and percentage loads are similar but different, both RPE and RIR are tools used to quantify how a set feels. However, RPE is measured on a scale, whereas RIR is measured in repetitions. As such, although there are similarities between the two, they are actually 2 different tools due to the simple fact that they are use different units of measurement.

Incorporating RPE and/or RIR Properly into Your Training

You now know that internal measures of stress are what cause adaptation and growth. Thus, external measures of stress, like prescribed loads with dedicated set and rep schemes, are merely attempts to create a specific training response. But since it is harder to capture the expected training response with external measures of stress, should we all be programming with internal measures of stress, like RPE or RIR, instead? No. Beginners, for example, may not be able to judge just how many reps they are still capable of performing, and even the best lifters struggle with predicting RIR until they approach failure. But, more importantly, programming with both percentage loads and RPE seems to be superior than using one over the other.

Back when RPE was all the rage in the world of powerlifting, a lot of coaches started using RPE to determine top sets of the day and percentage loads for back-off sets. For example, performing a triple at RPE 8 and then 3 sets of 3 at 80% of your triple may translate into a triple at 300 lbs followed by 3 sets of 3 at 240 lbs. This combination of RPE and percentage loads allowed for a brief exposure to a heavy load followed by a relative decrease in intensity to lighter loads. But during a recent Q&A, Mike Tuchscherer confirmed that it was better to set target weights for your top sets instead. [6] The question was as follows:

"[I still] feel like sometimes planned increases based on percentages are the most effective for me because everything always feels heavy and if I don't have that pre-determined number to hit I probably won't hit it simply using RPE. How do you advise your trainees who may be newer to the sport, or simply less driven or less confident to hit heavy weights to use RPE effectively as a tool to INCREASE working weights over time?"

To which Tuchscherer responded:

"I always advise everyone to use target weights. These are percentage based and designed to get you to the rep-RPE pairing for the day in most circumstances. Then you can go off plan as needed. [In my opinion], autoregulation functions best when it makes course corrections. Our autoregulatory tools [such as RPE] are not so good as to allow the entire program to emerge in an instinctive kind of way. They function best when we start with a very solid plan, then allow autoregulation to make course corrections." [6]

It seems that many coaches take this stance now too. The Strength Athlete, the powerlifting team that generally places second for best powerlifting team at IPF World's after Tuchscherer's Reactive Training Systems, has also recently updated their universal intermediate strength program to now use a top set based on percentage load too, instead of binding it to a RPE rating.

The New Faces of Volume

Volume, like percentage load, is also an external measure of stress. Unlike percentage loads though, volume tries to explain training stress over a span of time. For example, training volume for a certain exercise or workout is generally represented by poundage, which is the product of sets, reps and loads in lbs. However, volume as poundage fails to explain what kind of training stress is experienced by the lifter. For example, 2 sets of 2 at 500 lbs results in a poundage of 2000 lbs, but 3 sets of 20 at 50 lbs results in a poundage of 3000 lbs; although volume and poundage seem to be higher for the latter, it's more likely that the former scenario exerted more training stress. As such, many coaches have come up with new ways to quantify training volume, though not all coaches have opted for internal measures of stress.

How Boris Sheiko Calculates Volume as an External Measure of Training Stress

Boris Sheiko breaks down training volume into three different components: number of lifts (NL), poundage, and average intensity. While poundage is calculated no differently from how many other coaches calculate poundage, Sheiko calculates intensity as the average percentage load of all sets, including warm-ups, which differs from most coaches where only the percentage load of working sets mattered. Though if you've ever ran one of Sheiko's training routines you'd know why: The warm-ups beat you up and make the top sets feel brutal, despite looking easy on paper. For example, while most calculators and coaches estimate your 5-rep max to be about 87.5% of your 1-rep max, performing 5 sets of 2 at 80% as a working set on one of Sheiko's training programs can feel *extremely* challenging simply because you are already fatigued by the time you get to your working sets. Combined with number of lifts, the 3 compartments of volume – number of lifts, poundage and average intensity – answers what percentage loads you are building technical prowess at.

Though Sheiko calculates training volume through external measures of training stress, he also acknowledges the fact that internal measures of training stress matter – *a lot*. Sheiko has stated that: "Any plan, even one perfectly planned for a group of athletes and written by a highly accomplished coach, must be adjusted during training sessions. This is explained by the fact that athletes find themselves with different anatomical and physiological realities, and therefore they will have different reactions to load, different recoverability between workouts, and miscellaneous technique errors in the execution of competitive exercises." [27] So even though many people believe Sheiko's programs are to be followed exactly as written, his programs are actually meant to be adjusted as if they were written with RPE in mind.

Mike Tuchscherer's Training Stress Index

Like Boris Sheiko, Mike Tuchscherer also opted for an alternative to using poundage load when measuring training volume. But unlike Sheiko, Tuchscherer opted to quantify internal measures of training stress using his Training Stress Index, or TSI for short, which factors in actual training intensity. At the Powerlifting Summit 2017, Tuchscherer stated that poundage was flawed because 1) poundage can be artificially inflated by low intensity training efforts, such as accumulating a high poundage from a lot of low intensity work, which generally does not induce a lot of training stress or psychological fatigue; 2) poundage can be artificially inflated by mechanically advantaged efforts, such as very long arms that make training deadlifts a lot less fatiguing; and 3) poundage does a poor job at approximating the recovery costs of training, as a low poundage training session achieved through high load training gives off the impression that not a lot was done, yet in reality it could have been a very stressful training session.

$$Training\ Stress\ Index, TSI$$
$$= poundage\ \times psychological\ fatigue$$

Training Stress Index, TSI, is a product of poundage and psychological fatigue, which is approximated using RPE. For example, consider two lifters who are prescribed singles at 90%. A lifter who isn't used to high load training will both rate the sets higher on the RPE scale and accumulate higher psychological fatigue than a lifter who has been training at 90% recently. As such, TSI takes into account whether lifters have already adapted to a training stress or not. Tuchscherer found that psychological fatigue is closely related to recovery rate, hence why it is included in the formula for TSI.

You can calculate training stress by multiplying the total number of sets at each respective RPE by a stress coefficient. At the Powerlifting Summit 2017,

Tuchscherer provided the following RPE ranges and their respective stress coefficients:

RPE Rating	Stress Coefficient
5 to 6	0.5
6 to 7	0.667
7 to 8	0.8
8 to 9	1
9 to 10	1.33

The result is a number representing training stress. This training stress number determines 1) how difficult the training session was, and 2) how hard a week of training is. You can use the following tables from the Powerlifting Summit 2017 to understand your training stress number:

Training stress for movement/session		Training stress for a training week	
2.5	Easy session	14	Easy week
3.5	Moderate session	20	Moderate week
4.5	Hard session	26	Hard week

Note that neither stress coefficients nor training stresses are set in stone: You have to adjust these numbers for yourself. [6] For example, one of Tuchscherer's athletes, Liz Craven, can handle a training stress of 30 on a weekly basis despite being a 41 year old lifter at the time. However, other athletes would be on the brink of overtraining if they trained with a training stress of 30 on a weekly basis. Additionally, note that these numbers are very preliminary, and that you can get a cheat sheet for implementing TSI from www.andyxiong.com/bonus/realstrength.

So how would you make use of Tuchscherer's Training Stress Index in your training and programming? Think back to Project Momentum 2016, which revealed how well rested and how recovered you felt was directly related to gains and inversely related to injury rate. [14] Compared to poundage, the Training Stress Index is a much better indicator of how stressful training sessions can be and how much recovery is needed. For example, while it is possible to have low poundage with high training stress and vice versa, TSI will always be a consistent indicator of how stressful the training session was. You will never get a low stress index with a very stressful training session or week. As such, TSI is much better for regulating training volume as the stress index will be fairly stable for each individual lifter. In other words, if you are Liz Craven, so long as your training stress is around 30 per week, you can be sure that you are neither undertraining nor overtraining.

Robert Frederick's Exertion Load

Robert Frederick also has his own method of regulating volume and intensity, and he calls it Exertion Load. I've mentioned Frederick a couple of times already, but who is he? Although not as well known as either Boris Sheiko or Mike Tuchscherer, Frederick is actually a national Olympic strength coach mentored by Sheiko. He is also a top contributor to Sheiko's English forums. Thus, he is the top source for everything Sheiko-related for the English-speaking population.

Frederick's Exertion Load is very similar to Tuchscherer's Training Stress Index, and can result in very similar outputs too. However, there are some benefits to using Frederick's Exertion Load, though it comes at a cost of being slightly more complicated. In a 2018 Q&A, Tuchscherer stated that, "Robert Frederick wrote about Exertion Load. The outputs of his formula and my stress index are very, very similar. His has an advantage that it can be parsed out into central and peripheral [fatigue], which is nice." [6] However, being able to parse fatigue isn't as useful for strength athletes as it is for bodybuilders. As such, for simplicity's sake, I recommend implementing TSI instead.

For those who are interested in Exertion Load, it uses 4 variables: reps done, reps in reserve, range of motion and number of sets. However, when applied to strength training, Exertion Load is almost identical to Training Stress Index. How? For starters, range of motion is generally a constant in strength training, meaning Exertion Load really only uses 3 variables when applied to strength training. However, both reps done and reps in reserve can be also replaced by RPE for 2 reasons: 1) reps done is not as relevant to strength training as it is for hypertrophy purposes, and 2) RPE, like reps done and reps in reserve, is an indicator for intensity. Thus, the result is a formula with only 2 variables: number of sets and RPE, which is identical to the variables for calculating Training Stress Index! However, for those who are interested in implementing Frederick's Exertion Load, you can learn more from his website www.strongur.io.

As for why neither Frederick nor Tuchscherer includes mass in their calculations, Frederick states it best: "Why multiple by mass for each rep, as is traditionally done with volume load [or poundage]? That's conceptual baggage. We already have an indicator for intensity with Reps + RIR [or RPE]. If you do a squat with a heavier weight, your Reps + RIR value is lower [and your RPE is higher]. Done. Mass is redundant." [33]

Takeaways and Application

How you feel matters so much more than the actual numbers like load and volume. That's because you are training to get a specific training response, which is internal. External measurements such as the weight on a bar, poundage and reps, are only means of trying to attain a specific training stress. With many top coaches opting for newer, internal measures of training stress, we as lifters need to start caring more about how our training *feels* rather than the logic behind it. Mike Tuchscherer's Project Momentum 2016 confirms the importance of feeling recovered and well rested. [14]

Beginner lifters need not worry about applying these training variables, as their programming does not call for it. However, it can be a good idea to get into the habit of rating sets based on RPE as soon as possible, since more and more intermediate and advanced programs are starting to use RPE. Aside from RPE, while the other variables described in this chapter are generally important, you won't really be using them on a day-to-day basis unless you start writing your own programs. For example, while it's nice to understand how Boris Sheiko breaks down volume, you probably wouldn't need to use those variables unless you plan on modifying some of Sheiko's programs. Tuchscherer's Training Stress Index can prove useful however, as it allows you to gauge weekly training stress.

As a takeaway, *how we feel in response to our training is perhaps one of the most important training variables*. While variables like intensity and volume are at the forefront of training, there are also other training variables that are often forgotten. Yet, these forgotten variables are also some of the most important ones. In the next chapter, we talk about 2 of the most important, yet forgotten, training variables and how you can optimize them. Keep reading.

Chapter 8:

Training Variables – The 2 Most Important Yet Forgotten Training Variables

How you feel matters so much more than the actual numbers like load and volume. That's because you are training to get a specific training response, which is internal. External measurements such as weight on a bar, poundage and reps, are only means of trying to attain a specific training stress. With many top coaches opting for newer, internal measures of training stress, we as lifters need to start caring more about how our training feels rather than the logic behind it. Mike Tuchscherer's Project Momentum 2016 confirms the importance of feeling recovered and well rested. [14]

While variables like intensity and volume are at the forefront of training, there are other training variables that are often forgotten. Yet, these forgotten variables are also some of the most important ones. While training variables like intensity and volume describe programs, these training variables describe *you*. In other words, these variables determine how strong *you* are. While you can always hop onto different programs and adjust their training variables to fit your needs, it is these training variables that describe your needs in the first place. But before we get to these training variables, let's direct our attention to the most infamous variable of them all: Volume.

Shadowed by the Most Popular Training Variable, Volume

There is a lot of attention on volume, and rightfully so. Many of the strongest lifters and best coaches have stated that the strongest lifter is always going to be the one who has accumulated the greatest volumes of training. Of course, volume needs to be applied appropriately: You can't just hop onto a training program with the highest levels of volume at any given time. Doing too much volume when you are not ready for it can be detrimental. Thus, the most logical way to accumulate a ton of volume is to do it over longer periods of time, while also doing your best to avoid injury. As such, how much time you spend strength training will ultimately determine how strong you are. Experience matters.

Volume is also popular because it has been proven time and time again to be the driving factor for muscle growth and hypertrophy. A systematic review and meta-analysis performed by Greg Nuckols on his site, Stronger by Science, has suggested that volume is such a dominating factor for muscle growth that whether training is periodized or not, and how it is periodized, had little impact on muscle growth and hypertrophy. [24] A systematic review and meta-analysis published in the Journal of Sports Sciences in July 2016 by Dr. Brad Schoenfeld et al. also found a direct relationship between volume and muscle growth, with each additional set adding about a 0.37% gain in effect size. [34] This is echoed by other experts, like Dr. Austin Baraki, who stresses the importance of increasing training volume in order to build muscle mass. [5] Long story short, it seems that volume is directly related to muscle growth. And because muscle mass is related to strength, volume is also indirectly related to strength. No wonder volume is so infamous:

It encompasses everything training related, from muscle to strength!

But volume is an external measure of training stress, one that attempts to quantify training stress over larger spans of time, such as the span of multiple sets, entire training sessions, weeks, months, or even training cycles. But what internal measure of training stress does volume attempt to quantify? Robert Frederick states that volume is a proxy for measuring effort. [32] That means being able to tolerate increasing volume levels means being able to train with higher and higher levels of effort. In other words, volume and all of its derivations – like number of lifts, poundage, training stress, and exertion load – attempt to quantify training so that you can stay within your **work capacity**. Your ability to do work, known as work capacity, is the first training variable that is often overlooked. When you are increasing and adapting to higher and higher levels of volume, you are building up your work capacity. But if you have low work capacity and tire easily, or your recovery is slow, that's a weakness – not a strength. As such, your goal from the first day you step foot in the gym, even before building muscle, is to increase your work capacity.

Volume, for all the attention it gets, *is* important. It is important because it cumulates all of your training into work. And whether all this work is within your work capacity will determine whether a training program is too high volume for you and will cause overtraining, or too low volume for you and cause detraining. You should know by now how important volume is for muscle growth, and how important muscle growth is for strength. Thus, you should also understand the importance of building up your work capacity over time. Of course, we can't all be Liz Craven with over 150% of the work capacity of Mike Tuchscherer's average clientele, but we should all strive to build our work capacity up to its highest potential.

The Training Variable that Lost Its Meaning

Now that you know the first of 2 of the most important yet forgotten training variables, let's talk about the second: **Motivation**. I've already stressed the importance of how you feel in the previous chapter, yet none of the training variables at the forefront of training – volume load as poundage, intensity as percentage load, and frequency – considers how you feel. Motivation, though, is *all about how you feel.* I have to give credit to Jonnie Candito of Candito Training HQ for this, as he explicitly states that motivation is a training variable in his free beginner linear progression program Candito LP. Candito has been claiming this since 2014, when few coaches even considered things like motivation and internal measures of training stress.

However, the motivation I'm talking about is not the motivation you need to get your foot in the gym; you should already have gotten into the habit of working out consistently. In fact, the moment you started strength training was the moment you stopped needing motivation to work out for the sake of exercising. No: This is the motivation to keep striving to become better and stronger. You can always default onto the habit of working out in order to work out, *but you can't default onto anything if you don't want to improve in the first place.* Trust me, I've been there myself: Once the drive to improve is gone, you may continue training but you likely won't be progressing. In fact, this drive to improve will be the biggest roadblock to both your rate of progression and your gains.

How can you always remain motivated and driven to improve though? Or, how can you at least prevent motivation from dropping too much, to the point where progression is stopped? To answer these questions, we have to turn towards the field of self-help. Dr. Maxwell Maltz calls motivation or drive "life force," as it separates those who are old and fragile and those who are old in age but young in body, mind and soul. Others may consider it the will to live – not to be alive, but to actually *live* and achieve something. Regardless of what motivation and drive is, it all starts with having a goal. Dr. Maltz proposed that all humans are goal-strivers and that life force is what drives us forward towards our goals. But when we don't have goals, there's a problem: In his best-selling self-help book, *Psycho-Cybernetics*, Dr. Maltz wrote that "a stored automobile needs no gasoline in the tank. And a goal striver with no goals doesn't really need life force." No wonder Greg Nuckols and Mark Rippetoe suggest competing in powerlifting: It provides you with both strength and training goals; and you *need* goals.

To many, it can be making certain lifts, such as my pursuit of a 500 lb squat. It can also be certain totals, like joining the 1000 lb club, where your powerlifting total consisting of your squat 1-rep max, bench 1-rep max and deadlift 1-rep max total 1000 lbs. It can also be a certain Wilks score, or certain number of medals. To others, it can be winning local powerlifting meets, or even international competitions. It can be something as simple as being stronger than a friend or rival, or something grand like being the best of the best. There are also body composition goals, like having abs, or reaching your maximum muscular potential – which all intermediate lifters should strive for anyways. And if you're an advanced lifter, you can always strive for technical mastery. Heck, it can even be other forms of strength, like flexibility or strength at end range, which can potentially help with neuromuscular efficiency by allowing you to execute the same technique a lot easier and effortlessly.

The numbers are endless, and these are only some ideas of goals for you on your journey to becoming stronger. Yet, the lack of goals is also why most intermediate lifters give up on their strength journey in the first place: Many intermediate lifters care only about their squat, bench, deadlift and overhead press, and when they are no longer making progress – usually because they put all of their attention into specificity and technical mastery instead of muscle hypertrophy – they lose hope and feel defeated. The core of the problem is simple: If you define strength as force production, your goals will be very specific to lifting. But if you changed how you define strength, you will not only have more goals but you will also be more driven. Why? Because a step sideways is a step forwards if you change your perspective. And moving towards goals, whether big or small, primary or secondary, directly or indirectly, will always be motivating. But it all starts with having goals – and lots of them, as they fuel your desire for growth.

Still stumped? Well here's a goal for you: Finish this book. Read on.

Chapter 9:

Training Variables – Movement Patterns and Exercise Selection

Many people overlook why they are doing certain exercises over others, yet exercise selection is one of the few training variables that you have control over. For example, brute strength exercises can help you build mental strength much more than they help with building technical prowess, which would benefit you if you were a weak but technical lifter. But there's just one problem: Just what training exercises are considered staples? Are the slow lifts – the squat, bench press, deadlift and overhead press – staples that you should be performing year-round? Or is it the movement patterns – squat-like movements, horizontal and vertical push, and hip hinge movements – that are staples? We can solve this dilemma by analyzing what the top coaches from various different industries recommend, as well as what each sport demands from their athletes.

The *Sport* of Powerlifting and the Big 3: The Back Squat, Bench Press and Deadlift

Let's start off with the sport of powerlifting since we are using powerlifting standards to classify our training advancement. However, we have already determined that neither powerlifting nor the Big 3 are good indicators of strength. Thus, powerlifting training – where emphasis is on raising our competition back squat, bench press and deadlift – is super specific to the sport of powerlifting. Though having astronomical 1-rep maxes is an indicator of strength, being strong is a lot more than that. Yes, a 500 lb bencher can probably put up 405 lbs for an easy triple, but in the words of Mythical Strength's Emevas, *powerlifting is not the sport of getting strong*. It's a sport, and people tend to forget that. Emevas stated that "a strong powerlifter is going to have a solid shot at winning... but that's not the only thing a powerlifter needs. A powerlifter needs to also be SKILLED, both at the execution the lift (to include all the various powerlifting tricks regarding reducing [range of motion] as much as possible while aligning oneself into the best position to maximize leverages) and at the ability to handle maximal poundages. In addition, a powerlifter needs to know how to peak for a meet," whereas *you* don't (unless you are an advanced lifter who has specialized into powerlifting). [35]

Competition Lifts in the Sport of Powerlifting (The Big 3)		
Barbell Back Squat	Barbell Bench Press	Barbell Deadlift

I want to stress again that powerlifting is a sport, and sports have rules that can change over time. In fact, the biceps curl was once a competition lift in some federations, until it was replaced by the deadlift. Additionally, different powerlifting federations have different rules, just like how different countries have different classification standards. Some powerlifting federations allow for the use of suits, different barbells for each lift, and other equipment like knee wraps. Other federations require the feet and the head to remain in contact with the floor and the bench respectively for the entirety of the bench press; other federations only require your toes to be in contact with the floor. Bench presses are also paused and hitching isn't allowed on the deadlift, making powerlifting a rather technical and specific sport.

Conventional Strength Training and the Slow Lifts

Strength training as we know it – with emphasis on the squat, bench press, deadlift and overhead press – exploded in popularity thanks to Mark Rippetoe. Like powerlifting, the slow lifts are great ways to display strength, but it's not the only way of developing it. In fact, if it weren't for the concurrent growing popularity of both powerlifting and barbell strength training, the greatest appeal of conventional strength training with the slow lifts is how easy it is to get started: All you need is access to a barbell, a rack, a bench and some plates. It's a cheap investment compared to gym memberships, adding to its accessibility.

The Slow Lifts			
Squat	Bench Press	Deadlift	Overhead Press

But what if everyone had access to an infinite amount of resources, with every implement and training equipment available to them for free and without much travel? Would the slow lifts still be as popular as it is today for building strength? Probably not, as many strength enthusiasts and strongman competitors actually prefer other lifts for developing strength. For example, YouTuber and Strength Camp founder Elliott Hulse lists front squats, weighted dips, deadlifts and pulls ups as his 4 fundamental exercises for building strength [36]. Note that these exercises train the same movement patterns as the slow lifts – squats, deadlifts, pressing and pulling. This again begs the question: Is it exercises or movement patterns that we should be training?

Strongman Events and Training

Before we answer that question, I want to first touch on how strongman competitors train, as most treat their training as an extension of conventional strength training. According to Justin Lascek of 70's Big, strongman competitions consist of at least the following events: a carrying event, a pressing event, an event involving hip extension, and an event that requires loading something over a bar or to a platform. Occasionally, there's also a pushing and/or dragging event involving the use of sleds, prowlers or trucks. [37] Note that although these are the main category of events, the specific events – how heavy the implements are going to be, the exact implements being used, and whether it's a 1-rep max event or max reps event – aren't revealed until much closer to the event. As such, unlike powerlifting where you can practice how you play yearlong, strongman *training* is not as specific to strongman *competitions*. This means that strongman competitors have to train a variety of movement patterns, and be strong in more ways than one – something that we want to pursue as well.

Strongman Events	Examples
Walking or Carrying Event	Yoke walk, farmer's carries, etc.
(Vertical) Pressing Event	Log press, axle press, etc.
Hip Extension Event	Deadlift variations (axle, bar, car), tire flips
Loading (over a bar / to a platform) Event	Atlas stones, sandbags, etc.
Occasionally: Dragging/Pushing Event	Sleds, prowlers, trucks, etc.

Since our goals are similar, we should look towards how strongman competitors train in their offseason. Though different strongman competitors tend to train in different ways, at the simplest, strongman training consists of 4 fundamental movement patterns, and they happen to be the ones that make up the slow lifts. The fundamental movement patterns trained by strongman competitors are push, squat, deadlift and pull. This is evident with Elliott Hulse's list of fundamental strength exercises as previously mentioned. Another strongman competitor, Brian Alsruhe of Neversate Athletics, also train using those 4 movement patterns. However, Alsruhe tends to incorporate a lot more strongman implements, such as squats with a safety squat bar, axle bar bench presses, and log presses.

Mythical Strength's Emevas, a powerlifter and strongman competitor, argues that the slow lifts aren't even necessary for developing strength. He suggests that strength enthusiasts who aren't powerlifting, or don't plan on powerlifting, to avoid the Big 3 –the barbell back squat, barbell bench press, and barbell deadlift – as these lifts are specific for competition and are unnecessarily technical for developing strength. [38] Instead of the Big 3, Emevas recommends squats using a safety squat bar with chains, weighted dips, and either block or mat deadlifts – all of which are easier on the joints, require more full body strength, don't beat up the body as much so that you can train harder and more frequently, and are much less technical. [39][40] These are what I consider brute strength exercises, as they allow you to grind harder without fear of injury and without technical prowess.

Other examples of brute strength exercises are the axle press, which is much easier on the elbow and much less technical than standard barbell overhead presses. Axle presses allow you to train the pressing movement despite nagging joints. As another example, consider squats with chains, which make the squat feel considerably lighter at the bottom than the top: This keeps the weakest position for most lifters, the bottom of the squat, challenging while making the strongest position much harder. Compared to regular squats, which is rather technical due to the most difficult position being coming out of the hole, squatting with chains is challenging throughout the entire movement. Lastly, consider weighted dips to failure, which is not as frightening as bench pressing to failure because you can easily hop off the dip bars instead of having a barbell crush down on you.

Functional, Sports-Specific Training and General Strength and Conditioning Work

Functional training, sometimes known as sports-specific training or general strength and conditioning, is actually dependent on what kind of team sport you play or what your day to day life encompasses. As such, functional training will differ from one person to another. However, there are some commonalities amongst how all functional training coaches, sports coaches, and strength and conditioning coaches train their athletes or clients. For starters, there is a lot more emphasis on multi-planar work, as the transverse and frontal planes are neglected relative to the sagittal plane. The American Council on Exercise defines sagittal work as forward and backward movement relative to an imaginary line that splits the body into right and left halves (which includes flexion, extension and dorsi- and plantar-flexion work); frontal work is defined as lateral movement parallel to the imaginary line that splits the body into left and right halves (such as adduction, abduction, scapular elevation and depression, and foot inversion and eversion); and transverse work is defined as rotational movement parallel to the waistline (movement patterns such as rotation, forearm pronation and supination, horizontal flexion and adduction, as well as horizontal extension and abduction). [42] Additionally, there is a lot more emphasis on unilateral work in functional training, which is often neglected and overshadowed by the bilateral work popularized with barbell training.

As for fundamental exercises, there are none. Instead, there are fundamental movement patterns, which seem to be built off of Dr. Vladimir Janda's work. So instead of squats, you have knee-dominant lower body exercises, horizontal push movements instead of the bench press, and hip-dominant lower body exercises instead of the deadlift. The full list of movement patterns varies depending on who you ask, and different coaches tend to prioritize different movement patterns, or even swap out what they think is important. However, most coaches tend to agree on the following fundamental movement patterns and suggest that they be trained yearlong: 1) a knee-dominant movement, 2) a hip-dominant movement, 3) a horizontal press, 4) a horizontal pull, 5) a vertical press, 6) a vertical pull, a core exercise and an explosive exercise. What's interesting here is that squats aren't mandatory. In fact, many sports coaches prefer unilateral knee-dominant exercises like the lunge and step ups over the bilateral barbell squat.

Pavel Tsatsouline's StrongFirst adds loaded carries, rotation and counter-rotation as fundamental movement patterns, though the latter 2 tend to fall under core work. [42] Dan John, an infamous strength and conditioning coach, lists the following as his fundamental movement patterns: push, pull, hinge, squat, loaded carries and core – which includes abs, obliques and glutes in the form of planks, anti-rotation and unilateral work. Note that neither StrongFirst nor John decided to separate the push and pull movement patterns into horizontal and vertical planes of motion, and that John always includes an explosive movement in his programming too.

Fundamental Movement Patterns	Strong First [42]	Dan John	Dr. John Rusin [43][44]
	Loaded Carry	Loaded Carry	Loaded Carry
Knee-dominant	Squat	Squat	Squat
			Lunges
Hip-dominant	Hinge	Hinge	Hip Hinge
Horizontal Push	Push	Push	Horizontal Push
Vertical Push			Vertical Push
Horizontal Pull	Pull	Pull	Horizontal Pull
Vertical Pull			Vertical Pull
Core	Rotation, Counter-Rotation	Abs, Obliques, Glutes	
Explosive		Explosive	

Dr. John Rusin's list of fundamental movement patterns include squats, hip hinges, vertical and horizontal push movements, vertical and horizontal pull movements, carries and lunges. [43] What's interesting to note is that Dr. Rusin lists both squats *and* lunges, which are both knee-dominant lower body exercises, yet also considers single-leg hamstring work like the one-legged Romanian deadlift as a lunge. And although Dr. Rusin gives good reasons for why some of the movement patterns are fundamental – such as loaded carries for testing the pillar complex (the shoulders, hip and core), and the hip hinge due to 45 different muscles connecting to the hip – he gives no real reasoning as to why he includes both lunges and squats. The most logical reason I can come up with is that, to him, lunges meant unilateral leg work. [44] However, what's also interesting to note is that the horizontal push is primarily for judging shoulder health, and as such is best tested with banded pushups. The bench press, which many people consider to be the bread-and-butter horizontal pushing movement, is actually inferior for testing shoulder health, primarily because many people utilize leg drive to get the weight up.

Analysis of Fundamental Exercises and Movement Patterns

So what does this tell us? The more general the sport or training, the more varied it is. And if we're after strength in the most general sense, our training will have to be varied too. Real strength is about resilience and adaptability, after all. Since powerlifting training, which is specific to the sport of powerlifting, places a ton of emphasis on the Big 3 competition lifts, it cannot be the best way to develop strength as how we define it. On the contrary, though strongman competitions are made up of mainly 5 events, loads and events are actually unpredictable, and how strongman competitors train reflect this: Their training is a lot more varied. Instead of having fundamental exercises, strongman trainees practice variations of the same movement patterns. Functional, sports-specific and general strength and conditioning training is super general and covers a lot of different movement patterns, and drops fundamental exercises entirely for fundamental movement patterns. For example, whereas deadlifts may be considered a fundamental exercise for powerlifting and traditional strength training, strength and conditioning coaches may or may not use it to build the hip hinge movement pattern; to them, the movement pattern is more important than the exercise itself.

At its most general, strength training is about the ability to overcome challenges. Anything that challenges *you* can be considered strength training. To some, the Bosu ball squats prescribed by the personal trainers at your local gym *can* be a strength training exercise. Practicing new ranges of motion, new exercises, new motor patterns or even undergoing training for a completely new sport, can and will help you develop strength. And unless you are pursuing technical mastery in a few select lifts, incorporating new movement patterns will always benefit you. However, because we know what our goal is – real strength, in the most absolute and general sense – we can select and identify the specific movement patterns that we should focus on. This is because we've broken down strength into 3 factors: neuromuscular efficiency, muscle mass and the various physiological and psychological aspects of strength, such as mental strength and being free of imbalances and injuries. Movement patterns or exercises that neglect any one of these cannot be considered fundamental to *us*. I put emphasis on us because nothing is universally right or wrong – there's only right or wrong for *us*. Others, like powerlifters, will have different fundamental exercises and movement patterns.

My Fundamental Movement Pattern Recommendations

It can be daunting to try and figure out which exercises or movement patterns can be considered staples of training. Heck, different coaches have different ideas and recommendations. However, for strength enthusiasts like you, this can be simplified using 2 criteria:

1. The movement pattern and its exercises must build strength but, more importantly, it must also build size because how much muscle mass you carry is one of the greatest indicators of how strong you are. Thus, although many coaches recommend incorporating rotational work, this movement pattern trains primarily small muscle groups and will not add a ton of muscle mass onto your frame. Of course, you should still incorporate rotational work into

your training, but you can't really program a whole training day based entirely on rotational work and expect it to build a ton of muscle...

2. And that's the second criterion: The movement pattern should be important enough to be dedicated its very own day for training. Or, in other words, training the fundamental movement pattern should produce a ton of stress, to the point where it simply can't be trained with utmost intensity on a daily basis. So although core work is important, it's not important enough for people to go out of their ways to program a core day in their routine, and core work can actually be done on a daily basis, meaning it can't be a fundamental movement pattern for our training purposes. Again, you *will* end up performing core work, and every day too, as you will see in the next chapter.

Thus, our fundamental movement patterns will be as follows: a push, a pull, a knee-dominant movement, a hip-dominant movement and a loaded carry.

Note that these are movement patterns and not exercises. Thus, for the push movement pattern, it can be any pushing or pressing exercise – whether horizontal, like the bench press, or vertical like the overhead press. It can even be at an angle, like the weighted dip or incline press. In fact, I see little reason to separate the pushing movement pattern into horizontal and vertical planes. Unless your goal is to test or strengthen your shoulders independently of leg drive as Dr. John Rusin suggests, you can build healthy and strong shoulders using either horizontal or vertical pressing movements. Glenn Pendlay, renowned American Olympic Weightlifting coach, has his beginner weightlifters build shoulder strength primarily through the bench press – and yet, Olympic weightlifting is a sport where the barbell ends up overhead in every lift. In fact, Pendlay's athletes only practice the overhead press if they have trouble with getting and keeping the barbell in the overhead position. [45] Similarly, Dr. Mike Israetel, respected bodybuilder and bodybuilding coach, suggests that the overhead press, one of the best exercises for building the front of the shoulder, is *not* needed if you are already benching, as the bench press itself provides adequate shoulder growth. And since the bench press is a staple for chest growth, Dr. Israetel's clients are probably doing next to no vertical pressing for bodybuilding purposes. [46] As for powerlifters, where the goal is to maximize how much you can bench press, Jonnie Candito did not overhead press for the longest time yet still managed to bench press well over 300 lbs despite weighing less than 183 lbs. And when Mike Tuchscherer was asked about vertical pressing as assistance work for the bench press and for overall shoulder health, he stated that "some people find it effective. Some don't. I see the same thing in the people I coach." [6]

So whether you want to separate the fundamental movement pattern of pushing and pulling into different planes depends on your goals. For the most part, horizontal pressing is superior for strength and size, but if your sport demands vertical pressing you might want to consider incorporating both planes. General strength trainees who don't know what to specialize in should incorporate both horizontal and vertical pressing, but Mark Rippetoe's claim that the overhead press is necessary for shoulder health is unproven; as long as you bench press *properly*, your shoulders will remain healthy. Strongman competitors should also incorporate both horizontal and vertical pressing, as vertical pressing is a main event in strongman competitions whereas horizontal pressing is superior for strength and size development, primarily due to that fact that you can train it with heavier loads. Crossfit and Olympic weightlifting athletes would benefit from horizontal pressing for shoulder strength and whereas vertical pressing *can* help with the overhead position, emphasis will be on other, more efficient methods of getting the barbell overhead. As for powerlifters and powerlifting enthusiasts, you can replace all your overhead pressing with horizontal pressing variations like the close-grip bench press, which offer more carryover to your main lift.

The same goes for the pulling movement pattern: Any kind of pulling exercises will train the pulling movement pattern. However, there does appear to be a difference between pulling in the horizontal and vertical planes. For example, while most people will benefit from a higher ratio of pulling to pushing, only horizontal pulling has been shown to be effective in order to combat the imbalances caused by excessive pressing. Why? As it turns out, it's not so much about the ratio of pushing to pulling exercises as it is about balancing internal and external rotation. And vertical pulling, like pressing movements, trains internal rotation. Thus, according to Dr. Rusin, to develop healthy shoulders you should be pulling 3 times as much as you push, with a 2:1 ratio of horizontal to vertical pulling. That means for every pushing or pressing repetition, you want to do 1 repetition of vertical pulling and 2 repetitions of horizontal pulling. [47]

Instead of squats as a fundamental exercise, we have the knee-dominant movement pattern instead. Truth is you don't have to squat. Though the squat may have made a name for itself as the "king of all exercises," it's not a mandatory exercise for either bodybuilding or strength training purposes. In fact, the leg press and lunges can be as effective as squats for muscle growth, and lunges even double as a stretch for the quadriceps. During a Q&A, someone asked Tuchscherer if they can focus on a movement other than the squat as they've been experiencing diminishing returns with a squatting frequency of 2 to 3 times a week, to which Tuchscherer responded, "The only reason (in my opinion) that you HAVE to squat is if you're a powerlifter. If that's not you and you want to do lunges... go for it." [6] Just because many people consider the squat as a basic human movement doesn't mean you need to be squatting 600 lbs; switch it up a bit with lunges or split squats instead, which can open up tight hip flexors that most strength trainees tend to have. Unilateral work like step ups can help too, as they have the potential to fix lower body imbalances.

The next fundamental movement pattern is the hip-dominant movement pattern. This can take the form of a hip hinge, such as a conventional deadlift, or a full hip extension, such as those performed with heavy tire flips. As stated before, there are 45 muscles that attach to the hip, which means that there is something fundamentally wrong with your body if you cannot perform a proper hip hinge or a full hip extension. The deadlift, especially from the floor, is considered by many to be a fundamental exercise, but it actually requires quite a bit of flexibility to be able to perform it properly. Thus, the deadlift is not really a fundamental exercise; it is the hip-dominant movement pattern that is fundamental.

Note that if you low bar back squat, *it may or may not be considered a hip-dominant movement depending on how much you hinge.* If your low bar back squat is primarily a hip hinge, try to learn how to perform some knee-dominant squats or your arsenal of knee-dominant exercises may be limited to lunges and split squats. Though there's nothing wrong with either exercise, it can be rather difficult to train low bar squats, hip hinges like deadlifts *and* full hip extension all at once, or make meaningful progress on them if the lifts are cycled. Olympic high bar back squats, Zercher squats, front squats and squats with the safety squat bar do not have this issue as they are primarily knee-dominant movements, so it may be a good idea to invest in a safety squat bar or to start practicing the Zercher squat.

The fifth and last fundamental movement pattern is the loaded carry, which is recommended by most strength coaches because of its unique ability to test whether the pillar complex, which consists of the shoulders, hip and core, is functioning as a cohesive unit. Additionally, it can help you identify whether your gait, or how you walk, is wrong. When trained heavy, through an exercise like the Yolk carry, the loaded carry is a full body exercise that rivals the deadlift in terms of how many muscles are utilized, making it a great exercise for full body development.

Fundamental Movement Pattern Recommendation				
Push	Pull	Knee-dominant	Hip-dominant	Loaded carry

Fundamental Movement Pattern Honorable Mentions

There are two movement patterns that deserve honorable mentions. The first is the anterior chain movement pattern, primarily with ab wheel rollouts, which Dan John recommends over squats in his Easy Strength program. John's Easy Strength program is a high frequency training program that trains the push, pull, hip hinge, loaded carry and anterior chain movement patterns every single day. However, as for why the anterior chain movement pattern replaces the squatting movement pattern, John states that 1) squatting everyday is too brutal and that a 400 lb squat is all you really need, and 2) the goal should be to "increase your hinge, and maintain your squat." So it's not so much that the anterior chain movement pattern is a fundamental movement pattern, but more so that it was included to balance out the posterior chain training.

The other movement pattern that deserves an honorable mention is the bridge or glute-dominant movement pattern, which Dr. Bret Contreras is a huge proponent of. And if it weren't for the fact that a full hip extension – which falls under the hip-dominant movement pattern – involved the glutes so much, the bridge or glute-dominant movement pattern would have indeed been a fundamental movement pattern. In fact, the primary function of the gluteus maximus *is* hip extension. Thus, so long as you don't limit yourself to hip hinges such as deadlifts and include hip extension exercises in your training, listing the bridge or glute-dominant movement pattern as a fundamental movement pattern is redundant. However, many powerlifters and strength athletes *do* limit themselves to the hip hinge movement pattern via the deadlift, and that explains why most of their knee pain or training faults (like the knees collapsing inward during the squat) come from weak glutes. So keep in mind that the hip-dominant movement pattern involves both hip hinge *and* hip extension and you shouldn't need to bridge.

However, as I've mentioned several times already, there is no universal right or wrong: Thus, if you feel like bridging may benefit you, listing the bridge or glute-dominant movement pattern as a fundamental movement pattern is most definitely an option. When trained using heavy tire flips or hip thrusts, bridging and hip extension definitely qualifies as a fundamental movement pattern according to the criteria we set.

What about Core? – Anterior Chain, Plank, Rotation and Anti-Rotation Work

I've already covered why the anterior chain movement pattern is not a fundamental movement pattern, but neither are *any* of the core related movements; simply because they do not build enough muscle mass to justify dedicating an entire workout to them. While I will cover planks in the next chapter, I want to tackle whether we are even going to bother with rotation and anti-rotation work – and *how* if we are going to train them. Though StrongFirst includes rotation as one of its fundamental movements, I'd wager that it is because most strength sports and strength training methodologies completely neglect rotational work simply because of the fact that it isn't needed. Now if you're a powerlifter, it's true: You don't need rotational work. But we're not powerlifters and, because of how we define strength, we *are* going to include rotational work despite it not being important in many strength sports. However, we're not going to dedicate entire training sessions to rotational work: We are going to use it primarily for stretching and warming up. In fact, the spine loves rotational work, especially the thoracic spine. Although many people try to improve thoracic mobility by lying on a foam roller, thoracic mobility is actually best improved with rotations; though just make sure you are rotating at the spine and not the hip.

StrongFirst also lists anti-rotation as a fundamental movement pattern, and for good reason: Strength athletes, including powerlifters, actually incorporate anti-rotation work through core exercises like the bird-dog exercise. I like incorporating anti-rotation work a different way though, and to understand how you'll have to first understand why I didn't give an honorable mention to lunges as a fundamental movement, despite it being one of Dr. John Rusin's. And here's why: Dr. Rusin categorizes single-legged deadlifts under the lunge, so what he really means with the term "lunge" is unilateral leg work, which is actually great for fixing lower body imbalances and improving lower body strength. But unilateral work, although important, is actually anti-rotation work *provided that the unilateral exercise in question is a compound exercise that requires stabilization of the core.* For example, heavy 1-arm dumbbell presses, 1 arm TRX rows, contralateral lunges, and contralateral single-legged deadlifts are all unilateral compound exercises that also involve core stability, and as such can double as anti-rotation work. So as long as we incorporate compound unilateral exercises, we can end up checking off the boxes for anti-rotation work, unilateral work and, by extension, lunges.

What about Explosiveness and Explosive Exercises like the Olympic Lifts?

Power and explosiveness is much too varied to be considered a fundamental movement pattern: Taking any movement pattern and performing it explosively does not change the movement pattern itself. As such, it is like a layer that can be applied onto a movement pattern instead of being a movement pattern itself. Though not a fundamental movement pattern, we are still going to incorporate it into our training. In fact, explosive exercises are actually great exercises for warming up the body, muscle activation and getting the joints ready for movement. Kettlebell swings, for example, are an explosive hip hinge movement that can and should be used to warm up the glutes and hamstrings for lower body training.

But things get complicated when we attempt to classify the Olympic lifts. While such classifications have been made – Dan John classifies the clean and jerk as a pull, hinge, squat and loaded carry; the full snatch as a push, pull, hinge and squat; and StrongFirst claims "the snatch is a hinge, a pull, and a press all while controlling rotation" [48] – I would rather treat the Olympic lifts as their own unique movement patterns because of how specific they are. Heck, the only reason to perform the Olympic lifts is because your sport requires weightlifting. Whether it is for the Olympic Games or Crossfit Games doesn't matter; you are going to need to be good at both the snatch and clean and jerk. But if you want to train the Olympic lifts for the sake of training the Olympic lifts, or to be well-rounded, you should treat *triple extension* as a fundamental movement pattern instead. Triple extension, like the pillar complex, requires proper utilization and execution of multiple movement patterns and joints – primarily hip extension, knee extension and ankle plantar flexion.

But if you are only performing the Olympic lifts to develop power, you're no longer strength training – you're power training. Power (or power training) is not the same as strength (or strength training) because strength is a factor of power and power is an expression of strength. And since power training is not the same as strength training, I cannot give strength training recommendations for it. But also know that there is a lot of debate as to whether the Olympic lifts are even good for developing power, as many coaches believe that the Olympic lifts are too specific to the sport of weightlifting to be used as exercises to develop power capacity. Dr. Tudor Bompa, the father of modern sports periodization, states that "the Olympic lifting exercises are rigidly targeting only certain muscle groups, [and are] often not very important for many sports." Take judo for example, which is a sport that requires power and explosiveness. Dr. Bompa recalls, "I listened to a presentation regarding strength training for judo. The speaker was your typical Olympic lifting coach. He went over snatches and the clean and jerk! When the organizers asked my opinion, I simply said that the whole idea is wrong because judo involves primarily the flexor muscles of the hips, abdominals, and trunk, not the extensors normally targeted by Olympic lifting moves. The lifting coach became very upset when he heard me say this and left the room!" [3] Keep in mind that this is *before* we even get into proper weightlifting techniques like triple extension, which would make the exercises even *more* specific to the sport of Olympic weightlifting. However, like the kettlebell swing, the explosive nature of the Olympic lifts makes them a viable option for warming up and priming the body for training.

Putting It Together

Since you're probably thinking it, I'll say it: This chapter was a lot to take in. We covered a lot, such as why our 5 fundamental movement patterns are push, pull, knee-dominant, hip-dominant and loaded carries; why the glute-dominant and triple extension movement patterns are optionally fundamental; and why lunges, rotation, anti-rotation, anterior chain and explosive movements aren't considered fundamental, as well as how we plan to incorporate these non-fundamental but important movement patterns. But how do you fit all the various goals together into 1 cohesive training system? For example, how are we going to use loaded carries to not only test and prime our bodies so that we know our pillar complex is functioning properly, but also use it to build physical and mental strength *and* maximize hypertrophy? One requires the use of extremely light loads and technical mastery, while the other involves breaking form, overcoming your mental barriers, pushing yourself to your limits, and utmost training intensity. In the next chapter, I answer this question by showing you how to structure your workout. Read on.

Chapter 10:

The 4-Step Strength Training System

We covered a lot, such as why our 5 fundamental movement patterns are push, pull, knee-dominant, hip-dominant and loaded carries; why the glute-dominant and triple extension movement patterns are optionally fundamental; and why lunges, rotation, anti-rotation, anterior chain and explosive movements aren't considered fundamental, as well as how we plan to incorporate these non-fundamental but important movement patterns. But how do you fit all the various goals together into 1 cohesive training system? For example, how are we going to use loaded carries to not only test and prime our bodies so that we know our pillar complex is functioning properly, but also use it to build physical and mental strength *and* maximize hypertrophy? One requires the use of extremely light loads and technical mastery, while the other involves breaking form, overcoming your mental barriers, pushing yourself to your limits, and utmost training intensity.

Believe it or not, it is indeed possible to fit all of those movement patterns and goals into our training. That way, we can pursue and achieve the various goals concurrently as well as develop multiple facets of strength, all at once and all within one training cycle. How? We can structure our workouts in a way that includes everything we've covered. All you have to figure out is what exercises you are going to use for each fundamental movement pattern, and how many different movement patterns you want to train per workout. In fact, it is possible to apply what I'm about to show you with even beginner linear progression training programs like Starting Strength!

How to Structure Your Strength Training Workouts

Start off with whatever general warm up or activation exercises you would normally perform. For many, this may include foam rolling, monostructural work like biking or rowing, dynamic stretching and/or aggressive mobilization via banded distractions.

However, make sure to include rotational work for the spine and neck, and maybe even the hips. Rotational work can also double as stretching. In fact, most wrist and forearm stretches are rotational exercises in and of themselves. Then, you are going to implement the following 4-step training system, repeating it as needed for each fundamental movement pattern:

1. *Explosive-Activation*
2. *Regressive Plank*
3. Main Lift (*Strength* & *Hypertrophy*)
4. *Unilateral-Compound*

Step 1:
1 x 15-20 *Explosive-Activation*

Explosive-Activation exercises check off the need for explosive training. Explosive exercises, provided that they aren't too challenging, are great for activating and warming up muscle groups, and are also great at getting the joints ready for heavy lifting. Example exercises include kettlebell swings, push presses and jerks. If you follow Dr. Kelly Starrett, any Category 2 Movement from his book *Becoming a Supple Leopard* can work for *Explosive-Activation* since they all have the element of speed. This means wall balls, rowing, kipping pull-ups or kipping muscle ups, and jumping and landing are also options. (If you are baffled that I am recommending kipping movements, try and name one exercise that trains both global flexion *and* extension.) Regardless of what exercise you choose to perform, it should help activate the muscle groups needed for whatever fundamental movement pattern you are planning to train for the day. Perform your *Explosive-Activation* exercise for 1 set of at least 15-20 reps to prime your body for training.

Step 2:
Superset: 3-5 reps of *Regressive Plank*

After your *Explosive-Activation* exercise, you are ready to start training – but with supersets. You are going to superset what I call a *Regressive Plank* with your main lift. Your *Regressive Plank*ing exercise will be done at a low rep range of 3-5 reps, and with light loads because we're after technique. This allows you to prime and re-prime the movement pattern you are training before actually pushing yourself both technically and mentally on your main lift. For example, imagine that you are to perform 3x5

Olympic back squats this workout. Before every set of Olympic back squats, including warm up and working sets, you will perform 3-5 reps of a goblet squat. Use relatively moderate weights for your *Regressive Plank* (my max back squat is 450 lbs as of writing this book, and I use a 45-55 lb kettlebell for my goblet squats), and focus on performing the movement with mastery. The purpose of the *Regressive Plank* is to ensure proper functioning of the pillar complex for each fundamental movement pattern. For many, it may seem weird to superset your main lifts, but this is similar to the weightlifting technique of priming the body for something like the full clean through the use of hang cleans first.

For an exercise to qualify as a *Regressive Plank*, it must meet 4 criteria: It must be 1) a corrective exercise, 2) a regressive exercise, 3) a compound exercise that doubles as a plank, and 4) an assistance exercise to the main lift. It must be corrective and fix any bad motor patterns you may currently have, but calling it a corrective exercise is far too general: Almost any exercise can be a corrective exercise in one way or another. Fortunately, according to Dan John, regressions are the best and most efficient use of time in terms of corrective exercises. [49] This makes sense because regressions are, by definition, easier variations of a movement. For example, the push up is a regression of the bench press – the movement is the same but one is much easier to perform properly. And if the regressive exercise in question is a compound exercise involving the core, the regressive exercise will double as a plank. Planks, when done properly, require proper functioning of the pillar unit, such as proper alignment and stability, making it great for corrective purposes as it forces you to use your muscles and kinetic chains how they're meant to be used. Lastly, it must be an assistance exercise that *assists* the main lift; it shouldn't be the main lift itself. That's because if, for example, your squat is technically flawed, that technical flaw is probably what's holding you back. Thus, why would performing more of these incorrect squats fix the problem? Use exercises that are similar, in that they train the same movement pattern, but are different at the same time.

Examples of good *Regressive Plank*ing exercises are the goblet squat for the knee-dominant Olympic high bar squat and front squats, pushups for horizontal pressing and TRX rows for horizontal pulls, as these exercises meet all 4 criteria required of *Regressive Planking* exercises. The leg press, though it can be considered as a regressive compound exercise to the knee-dominant squat, does not utilize the pillar complex the same way the squat does – especially because there is no shoulder involvement in the leg press – so it is considered a poor choice.

Additionally, note that individuality matters here, so don't expect to find a list of regressions online and expect it to work flawlessly for you without first understanding how you yourself move. For example, Dr. Starrett suggests that the back squat is a regressive exercise to the front squat, whereas Dr. John Rusin suggests the contrary: That the front squat is a regressive exercise to the back squat. [44] Remember how I said that there is no such thing as universally right or wrong, but that there's a right or wrong for you? Well, who is right depends on how *you* squat: If you are a hip-dominant low bar squatter, the front squat will be more challenging to you and thus a knee-dominant back squat can be considered a regressive exercise to the front squat. If you are a knee-dominant squatter, the back squat will be more challenging to you, though not because it's a more technically demanding than the front squat but, solely because of how much heavier you can load the back squat.

Step 3:
Superset: Main Lift – *Strength & Hypertrophy* Exercise

For the most part, strength training *is* hypertrophy training, provided that the training stimulus is adequate. There is actually a lot of overlap between strength training and training for muscle growth, and it only fails to hold true at training extremes like sets of 20+ reps. [32] Even exercise-wise, some of the best exercises for developing strength, like the squat, bench, and deadlift, are also some of the best hypertrophy exercises. Even Dr. Mike Israetel states the best exercise for growing the quadriceps is indeed deep squats; for the chest, incline and flat bench presses; for the front of the shoulders, the overhead press; and for hamstrings, the conventional deadlift. [50]

However, your main lift must meet 2 criteria to be considered your *strength & hypertrophy* exercise: It must be 1) a compound exercise, and 2) it must train one of the fundamental movement patterns. Isolation exercises do not build full body strength. Aside from those 2 limitations, your main lift can be anything you please so long as it trains one of the fundamental movement patterns. It can even be a unilateral exercise like the lunge. Ultimately, your training advancement and your current weaknesses should determine what exercises will make up your roster of *strength* & *hypertrophy* exercises. Think of how Mike Tuchscherer classifies exercises into General, General-Specific and Specific exercises, with the latter being more specific to the sport you are competing in. Depending on what you are trying to achieve, there's a time and place for *every* kind of exercise.

For example, if you are strong with bad technique, your goal should be building technical prowess. Thus, train using exercises specific to your goal or sport. This will allow you to work on neuromuscular efficiency and build the muscles that are required of the movement. If you are weak but have good technique in the exercises that matter to you, you will need to train different movement patterns to combat specificity and become better-rounded and mentally stronger. In *Practical Programming for Strength Training*, even Mark Rippetoe stated that "strength and power are best acquired in ways that best develop strength and power, not in ways that strength and power are applied on the field." Thus, consider incorporating brute strength exercises, which are General to General-Specific strength training exercises where you can grind more safely and without fear; and because they are different movements in and of themselves, you don't have to worry about carrying over bad motor patterns to your main lifts. In previous chapters, I've stated that Elliott Hulse recommends front squats, weighted dips, rack pulls, and the push press, while Emevas of Mythical Strength suggests squats with a safety squat bar and chains, block or mat pulls, and weighted dips. However, my personal favorites are exercise variations that use either the bamboo or earthquake bar, which bring out both muscular and kinetic chain weaknesses. Earthquake bench press, for example, points out where you are lacking stability and leaking power. To combat the oscillating kinetic energy, your body is forced to use muscles that you commonly neglect, and thus are weak, in order to make the lift. The result is not only an exercise that pinpoints all of your technical flaws, but it also corrects it while training the muscles that you normally neglect. If you don't have access to an earthquake bar, a similar effect can be emulated by tying kettlebells to a standard barbell using resistance bands.

Step 4:

1-2 Sets of *Unilateral-Compound* Exercises

After your main lift, you are going to perform 1-2 sets of unilateral work that trains a similar movement pattern to your main lift. Note that this is 1-2 sets per *side*. Additionally, your choice of exercise must meet 2 criteria for it to qualify as what I call a *Unilateral-Compound* exercise: 1) it must be unilateral or asymmetric, meaning you are training one half of your body at a time, and 2) it must be a compound exercise that makes use of your core. If these 2 criteria are met, your *Unilateral-Compound* exercise will double as core work, due to the anti-rotational strength required, and as unilateral work. So while the single arm TRX row, single arm dumbbell bench or overhead press, and contralateral lunges are exercises that qualify as *Unilateral-Compound* exercises, the single-legged leg press does not because neither core strength nor anti-rotation is used, tested or trained with the leg press.

Bodybuilding, Stretching, Conditioning and Cardio Work for the 4-Step Training System

The 4-step training system can be summarized as such: Start with *Explosive-Activation*, then perform supersets consisting of a *Regressive Plank* with your *Strength & Hypertrophy* exercise, then conclude your strength work with a *Unilateral-Compound* exercise. After that, you can opt to repeat the process for another fundamental movement pattern if you are training multiple movement patterns on the same day, move onto bodybuilding work, or call it a workout. For examples of the 4-step training system I've personally used, head onto www.andyxiong.com/bonus/realstrength.

4-Step Training System Examples		
Movement Pattern	Knee-Dominant	Push
Explosive-Activation	Kettlebell Swings	Push Press
Regressive Plank	Goblet Squats	Push Ups
Strength & Hypertrophy	Front Squats	Bench Press
Unilateral Compound	Pistol Squats w/ Kettlebell	1-Arm Dumbbell Bench

However, you should already know by now that increasing your training volume and work capacity are important to continuously grow stronger. Thus, I highly recommend always performing bodybuilding work, either at the end of your workouts or on your rest days. Greg Nuckols even states that, for intermediate lifters, most of your training volume should come from assistance exercises, like variations of your main lifts and bodybuilding isolation exercises. [4] I recommend bodybuilding isolation exercises over variations, mainly because they are less taxing on the body and won't impact your strength training as much as variations. Additionally, training with isolation exercises allows you to better develop your mind-muscle connection, which is key for muscle growth. At the same time, isolation exercises can be done with utmost intensity with little to no consequences, and this high intensity training is what builds mental strength. The worst that can happen with high intensity isolation training is maybe delayed-onset muscle syndrome, whereas repeatedly pushing compounds to failure can result in some serious injuries. Big compound exercises, according to Jim Wendler, should stress the mind and joints, whereas small isolation exercises should be used to stress the muscles.

Make sure to train muscle groups that tend to be neglected. For most general strength athletes, this tends to be the biceps, calves, neck, forearms, posterior deltoids, lateral deltoids and maybe even the upper traps. Stretching, which is in many ways similar to bodybuilding, should also be performed at the end of your workouts. Conditioning and cardiovascular work, which should be done with high intensity to build mental strength, can also be used to increase your work capacity. And for those of you who would rather call it a day after your fundamental strength work, I want you to dwell on this question: If you aren't doing bodybuilding accessories, stretching at the end of your workouts and doing conditioning work, are you *truly* building comprehensive strength? Are you becoming more adaptable, capable and resilient, or are you only chasing strength as force production?

ANDY XIONG

Conclusion

Strength training is more than increasing quantifiable expressions of strength. Though your 1-rep max may be a good indicator of how much force you can produce against a resistance in the form of a barbell, defining strength as such is much too specific to lifting. *Resistance can exist outside of the gym*, and as such strength must be redefined. Of course, that doesn't change the fact that weight lifting is still one of the best ways to go about building strength. However, problems arise when you go about building strength with only force production in mind. For starters, the factors of strength and force production that cannot be changed, like your genetics, are super specific to lifting, meaning the playing field may not be as level as you want it to be. And most strength training programs emphasize mastering only *one* factor of strength, which just so happens to be the one most specific to lifting – technicality via neuromuscular efficiency. Yet, there are other factors of strength that contribute more to both who you are and what you are capable of.

And from examining how the best strength and powerlifting coaches train their athletes, we can observe the rise of new training variables; training variables that measure internal stress. In other words, *how we feel matters a lot*. So you shouldn't train one way just because it is "logically" the best way to go about training, or because it's how powerlifters or strongmen that you look up to train. Your training should be specific to *you*, how *you* feel, *your* training advancement, *your* goals and *your* weaknesses. We shouldn't train using the same exercises yearlong because that's what others do; we need to explore new exercises while perfecting the fundamental movement patterns that matter to *us*.

So what should you do? Figure out your training advancement and realize what your macro training goal is. For intermediate lifters, that's filling your frame with muscle, but don't hammer at it in the most direct way possible: You still need to fix what is specifically holding *you* back, whether that's bad technique or just overall weakness. With these 2 in mind, you can find a training methodology that works for you, and implement the 4-step training system to encompass all factors of strength in your programming. For example, you can opt for Jim Wendler's 5/3/1 system for your strength and hypertrophy exercises, while implementing our 4-step training system and training the movement patterns fundamental to you. But don't forget the other factors that make you strong too. If you feel tight, stretch so that you feel good instead; if you feel fat, cut because it's not so much about body mass as it is about *muscle* mass; if your training feels easy, make it harder so that it builds mental strength using autoregulation tools like RPE and TSI; if you feel like you've lost the motivation to improve, take a step sideways and find new goals. Most importantly, eat a healthy diet and get adequate rest so that you *feel* good, because how you feel has a huge impact on both your gains and whether or not you will get injured.

At the end of the day, strength is not about doing; it's about being. But as long as you define strength as force production, you will identify yourself by how you train and what you do. But an identity is who you *are*, not what you do. And as long as you define strength as force production, strength training will never do anything for your character, and you will never end up working towards becoming a better and more confident version of *you*.

References

1. https://www.facebook.com/story.php?story_fbid=10156130876498779&id=505233778

2. https://forum.barbellmedicine.com/forums/training-q-a-with-dr-jordan-feigenbaum-and-dr-austin-baraki/9931-have-i-got-the-idea

3. https://www.bodybuilding.com/fun/mahler18.htm

4. https://www.strongerbyscience.com/complete-strength-training-guide/#Why_some_people_lift_more_and_others_lift_less

5. https://www.exodus-strength.com/forum/viewtopic.php?p=73291#p73291

6. https://www.exodus-strength.com/forum/viewtopic.php?f=36&t=1539

7. https://www.strongerbyscience.com/unleash-your-inner-superhero/

8. https://www.strongerbyscience.com/genetics-expectations/

9. https://rd.springer.com/article/10.1007/s40279-018-0872-x

10. https://www.facebook.com/story.php?story_fbid=10215610143235484&id=1498006393

11. https://www.coachpapayats.com/chinese-weightlifting-blog/chinese-pull-vs-american-pull

12. https://www.catalystathletics.com/article/129/Six-Truths-of-Olympic-Weightlifting-Technique/

13. https://stronglifts.com/5x5/#321553215312153

14. https://articles.reactivetrainingsystems.com/2016/04/01/project-momentum/

15. http://mythicalstrength.blogspot.com/2018/05/the-fighter-or-barbarian.html

16. https://exrx.net/Testing/WeightLifting/StrengthStandards

17. https://startingstrength.com/files/standards.pdf

18. https://barbend.com/strength-standards-strongman/

19. http://www.powerlifting.ca/qual_totals.html

20. http://forum.reactivetrainingsystems.com/content.php?35-The-Russian-Classification-Chart

21. https://www.jtsstrength.com/periodization-powerlifting-definitive-guide/

22. https://www.ncbi.nlm.nih.gov/pubmed/28848690

23. https://www.sciencedirect.com/science/article/abs/pii/S0765159717302137

24. https://www.strongerbyscience.com/periodization-data/

25. http://sheiko-program.ru/forum/index.php?PHPSESSID=46aolr784h4p6sf65e4ag2eoq5&topic=311.0

26. https://www.ncbi.nlm.nih.gov/pubmed/27328853

27. http://sheiko-program.ru/the-basics-of-sheiko-by-robert-frederick

28. https://old.reddit.com/r/powerlifting/comments/36ihrj/the_basics_of_sheiko/crer3pp/

29. http://forum.reactivetrainingsystems.com/content.php?83-Learn-to-Grind

30. https://rd.springer.com/article/10.1007/s40279-018-0872-x

31. https://articles.reactivetrainingsystems.com/2017/05/10/project-momentum-17-1-results/

32. http://www.strongur.io/monitoring-training-stress-with-exertion-load/

33. http://www.strongur.io/using-exertion-load-to-predict-metabolic-stress/

34. https://www.ncbi.nlm.nih.gov/pubmed/27433992

35. http://mythicalstrength.blogspot.com/2018/04/size-not-bodybuilding-strength-not.html?m=1

36. https://www.youtube.com/watch?v=fIkoqmXWw

37. http://70sbig.com/blog/2011/12/strongman-training-for-beginners/

38. http://mythicalstrength.blogspot.com/2014/06/if-you-arent-powerlifting-why-are-you.html

39. http://mythicalstrength.blogspot.com/2014/04/training-movements-for-non-competitive.html

40. http://mythicalstrength.blogspot.com/2014/04/training-movements-for-non-competitive_21.html

41. https://www.acefitness.org/fitness-certifications/ace-answers/exam-preparation-blog/2863/the-planes-of-motion-explained

42. https://www.strongfirst.com/seven-basic-human-movements/

43. https://drjohnrusin.com/functional-strength-standards/

44. https://www.t-nation.com/training/the-6-foundational-movement-patterns

45. http://web.archive.org/web/20140421065134/http://www.pendlay.com/A-Training-System-for-Beginning-Olympic-Weightlifters_df_90.html

46. https://renaissanceperiodization.com/front-delt-training-tips-hypertrophy/

47. https://www.bodybuilding.com/content/safe-strong-upper-body-lifting-begins-with-these-two-ratios.html

48. https://www.strongfirst.com/pushing-better-pull/

49. https://www.t-nation.com/training/high-performance-no-bs-correctives

50. https://renaissanceperiodization.com/hypertrophy-training-guide-central-hub/

Made in the USA
Columbia, SC
11 November 2019

83095910R00111